On the Brink of Annihilation

How the Feminine Principle Can Save Us

ON THE BRINK OF ANNIHILATION

How the Feminine Principle Can Save Us

by

Gertrude Morin
and
Dr. Harold J. Breen

Huntington House Publishers

Printed in the
United States of America.

Huntington House Publishers
P.O. Box 53788
Lafayette, Louisiana 70505

Library of Congress Card Catalog
Number 99-61667
ISBN 1-56384-167-3

Contents

Not nature, but the genius of mankind has knotted the hangman's noose with which it can execute itself at any moment.

Carl Gustav Jung
Film, *Matter of Heart*

Acknowledgments

Dr. Breen, my coauthor, died on Good Friday while this book was in press. It stands as a tribute to his keen mind, sweeping intelligence, and compassionate understanding of the issues with which this study is concerned.

My thanks go to Veronica Tremblay for her accommodating work on the computer.

The enthusiastic encouragement and friendship of Dr. Malca Lebell and Nina Saab made a difference and were certainly appreciated.

Gertrude Morin

Introduction

This book is about unbalanced aggression and the human psyche. It is not a speculative work but based on hard reality. Today, people are becoming very fearful about undertaking the ordinary tasks of everyday life. From the time that we get up in the morning till we go to bed at night, we are anxious about the possibility of a destructive event taking place in our immediate vicinity. Such unease is certainly legitimate. One has only to turn on the television set for the latest "on the hour" news; not a day goes by without reports of murder, rape, child molestation, or bomb explosions in public places.

On a global scale this aggression, of course, takes the form of war, which is a danger to our species as a whole. From the beginning of recorded history, man has been a warring creature. He has been marvelously inventive as well. Both aspects are part of an aggressive "cutting edge" masculinity that has been vitally necessary, until now, for the survival of the human species. The danger is that we now live with the threat of total extinction by atomic warfare which hangs over us like the sword of Damocles.

No one wants to face this terrifying reality, and yet it must be confronted if we are to survive as a species. It is all very well and comforting to think of atomic weapons as deterrents to war and protective insurance. But, recalling the fable about the emperor who wore no clothes, this attitude is tantamount to agreeing that the emperor is dressed when, in fact, he is quite naked. Getting beyond denial, one can all too readily imagine a situation in which another world war would take place, but this time with the use of atomic weapons. The holocaust would be unimaginable. It is only a matter of time before an event of this nature occurs, given the warring nature of man.

Hopefully, we can make a radical evolutionary leap in human emotional development before such a disaster overwhelms us. It is, therefore, necessary to get down to the very root of our being in order to assess our fundamental psychological makeup and to seek new direction. As Carl

Jung optimistically stated during an interview with John Freeman in 1949, "A great change of our psychological attitude is imminent. That is certain" (*C.G. Jung Speaking* 436). Asked *why*, he replied:

> Because we need more—we need more psychology. We need more understanding of human nature, because the only real danger that exists is man himself. He is the great danger, and we are pitifully unaware of it. We know nothing of man, far too little. His psyche should be studied, because we are the origin of all coming evil.

My coauthor (a psychoanalyst) and I, working with Jung's fundamental outlook and insightful contributions, have tried to address the challenge posed by this modern-day prophet. Our book provides an answer to the age-old problem of war. It is not an easy solution that confronts us at this stage. It is, however, a vitally necessary one. Without a radical change of heart, the human species faces a terrible and irredeemable end. Much as we would like to ignore this reality, we cannot afford to do so.

The facts that we present are not complex, nor are they material for academic discussion. As a wise American professor once said to his class, “I don’t know how to make the truth sound profound. It never does.”

"There will be violence in the streets."

Marta Wassermann, 1960s

Chapter One

Violence in the Streets

I remember a time when my mother, slipping into a cardigan, set out for an evening walk. Having finished with the constant domestic demands of the day, she looked forward to this peaceful solitary venture with great pleasure. She never thought of locking the door behind her. No one did then, for there was simply no need.

Gone are those peaceful days. As much as I might enjoy the exercise, there is no way that I feel secure enough to follow my mother's example. Today, women in the city do not dare to venture forth alone in the evening for fear of sudden violence. We now keep our homes and cars securely locked at all times, whether we are within or not. For many, simple locks offer insufficient safety, and we install elaborate alarm systems to warn us of human predators.

In the nineteen sixties, Marta Wassermann, a very wise Viennese psychoanalyst, saw what lay ahead. She predicted that there would be "violence in the streets." Who would have imagined then the accuracy of her forecast and the extent of violence in America today? Hardly a day goes by without a stabbing or killing, single or multiple, domestic or public, being reported on the news. We hear of women and young girls being raped, killed, and then dumped into ravines or rivers. While horrifying, it is no longer a novelty to hear of a lone gunman obliterating a classroom of innocent children or women.

Vanished is the sense of assurance that life will roll on peacefully as it did in the past. The other day, as I walked along a downtown street, a beggar asked me for some change. Afraid to open my wallet and chance being robbed I said "No—sorry." I walked away quickly, afraid that this man would pull a knife and stab me. In the past, such a thought would have been inconceivable, and fear would not have inhibited a natural inclination to charity.

Increasing our anxiety and unease is the recent phenomenon of domestic terrorism in America. In July, 1996, in the dead of night, a bomb exploded in Centennial Park during the Olympic games being held in Atlanta, Georgia. This catastrophe occurred despite intensive, elaborate security measures taken by government authorities. Two people died and over one hundred were injured. According to an FBI agent, the explosive was a crudely made pipe bomb stuffed with screws and nails that became shrapnel when it went off. Apparently the fragments, hurtling as far as one hundred yards, lodged in the bodies of park visitors enjoying a musical concert.

In the year before, one of the worst acts of domestic terrorism in U.S. history occurred with the bombing of the Alfred P. Murrah Federal Building in Oklahoma City. Hundreds of adults and children were wounded and killed. At the time, disbelief that a bombing could occur in the city numbed the population. One man expressed despair over his inability to attend all the funerals of his friends whose lives were lost in this disaster. The carnage and wreckage created by the bomb reminded observers of the buildings destroyed by bombers in World War II. War is, after all, one huge act of terrorism in which each side tries to intimidate the other by destroying their resources, human and otherwise.

Whether by criminal violence or domestic terrorism, Americans are under attack, and war rages within the confines of our own cities. The situation is rapidly getting out of control. This is not a strictly national phenomenon. Ordinary citizens all over the world are filled with fear of escalating aggression. Our political leaders, with the best of intentions, offer us peace of mind with promises to "fight crime," to "come down hard" on criminals, to "get very aggressive" with terrorists. Tough measures, however, will not work. The retaliatory principle of meeting aggression with aggression can be no more effective than fighting fire with fire.

We have to get at the root of the current disease in our society. In order to understand the source of our contemporary explosion of aggression and destruction, it is necessary to examine the psychology of war. It is at the global level that the ultimate danger lies—the permanent destruction of the entire human race and the agonizing suffering involved. The entire fabric of our society is in serious trouble, and the very future of civilization is at risk. Violence in the streets and domestic terrorism are merely individual manifestations of an extremely serious global crisis.

And towering over a darkened world is the ever-increasing threat of a world-wide atomic war. But as Jung says, it is not the bomb that is the danger but the psychology of the men who control it.

Eleanor Bertine, M.D.
Carl Jung, 1875-1961:
A Memorial Meeting, 1961

Let man but accumulate his materials of destruction and the devil within him will soon be unable to resist putting them to their fatal use.

C.G. Jung
Modern Man In Search of a Soul

Chapter Two

The Hangman's Noose

On a lovely, still, August morning in the city of Hiroshima, Japan, people went about their morning affairs. Wives and mothers prepared breakfast, men and women left for work, children were sent off to school. Suddenly, at 8:16 A.M., hell broke loose. There was a blinding flash of lights, a blast of searing heat followed by an ominous, multi-colored cloud rising like a gigantic mushroom into the sky, its flaming roots spreading with the devastating intensity of a tornado. A United States aircraft had dropped its secret weapon, the first atomic bomb. Nicknamed, *The Little Boy,* the bomb had an explosive power equivalent to thirteen-and-a-half thousand tons of TNT. Three days later, Nagasaki met a similar fate.

Within an instant, the bomb dropped on Hiroshima destroyed sixty thousand houses in a three-mile radius and left a burnt-out wasteland. Those closest to the epicenter of the bomb blast were incinerated on the spot. Others within a mile and a half radius of the explosion succumbed shortly after from flash burns and intense doses of radiation. Those not killed immediately could not fathom what had happened to them. Staggering about half naked, clothing ripped from their bodies, skin hanging in shreds, facial features melted beyond recognition, they thought they were in a Buddhist hell. Many lingered on for years, blind, disfigured, crippled, and dying slowly from radiation damage and cancer. The survivors were never certain about the damaging effects passed on to the next generation.

A youth who entered Hiroshima in search of his family on the afternoon following the bombing, saw a young mother with a baby on her back and a youngster clasped in her arms. Pinned against the girder of a bridge, her dead body bobbed in the gentle current. As he approached Hiroshima station, the young man found charred bodies buried in a welter of ashes, tiles and plaster. Here and there an arm or leg protruded. Other bodies lay on the surface, their stomachs torn open and their entrails pouring into the ashes. The expressions on the dead faces were contorted and agonized.

Skeletons of burnt streetcars were later found with their fire-blackened passengers, the odd corpse still clinging to a strap. Floating in the Kyobash River, where many had headed in an instinctive effort to douse their flaming bodies, were scores of corpses, some with grotesquely swollen faces and legs stiff as logs; others with upper bodies burned black, and the lower half swollen and waterlogged.

In retrospect, the nickname chosen by the Americans for the bomb, *The Little Boy*, was ironically apt. It was, in fact, a small child compared with the thermonuclear giants that have been developed since then which stand ready to demolish the entire human species, indeed, all life on this planet. As Carl Gustav Jung, the prophet of our crucial era, said in the 1952 film, *Matter of Heart:*

> Not nature, but the genius of mankind has knotted the hangman's noose with which it can execute itself at any moment.

According to the film, Jung, before his death, foresaw that the end of civilization as we know it would come around the turn of this millennium. Jung's daughter recorded his vision on paper and gave it to her father's colleague, Marie Louise Von Franz. The note was then placed in a desk drawer, which remained closed because of its distressing content.

Apocalyptic prophecies are not new or few, but Jung's forecast is not mere idle conjecture. Certainly, it will become a horrible reality if someone accidentally or willfully releases a nuclear arsenal, thus inviting a similar response from the targeted area. Viewed by world leaders as useful defensive deterrents to another world war (Winston Churchill called the first atomic bomb a "miracle of deliverance"), the destructive effects of today's nuclear stockpiles will hardly deter a psychotic, vengeful leader who is prepared to end his own life in order to bring ruin to his enemies. All that is required for such a disaster is a scenario of chaotic economic times similar to the post World War I era in Germany that brought Hitler to power; with another leader like Hitler in charge of his own nuclear arsenal, all life on this planet will surely be destroyed.

Understandably, most of us prefer to avoid thinking about this possibility, for it is painfully akin to an encounter with hell. Can we readily imagine a raging inferno, ignited by explosions tearing through all our lands? Clouds of black nuclear smoke would blanket the sky, eclipsing the sun. Temperatures, consequently, could fall to unbearably cold levels. Those of us not instantly vaporized or burned to ashes would have nowhere to hide, nowhere to go for relief. Water and food supplies would be contaminated and the air irreversibly poisoned. After the holocaust, darkness and cold might prevail and the entire earth would be lifeless, for without sunlight, flowers, trees, and all vegetation would die. Who would want to go on living on a scorched and barren earth, even if he or she miraculously survived in some underground shelter? In view of this prospect, it seems inconceivable that President Reagan, at one time, considered the feasibility of *limited* nuclear war! It is simply a matter of time before the aggressive ways of warring men release the weapons that will destroy all life on this planet. Catastrophe hangs by a thread.

History, to date, is a record of mankind moving forward in time through an endless, bloody process of war wherein nothing is ever really solved. As Margaret Atwood has written in her novel, *Cat's Eye,* "An eye for an eye merely leads to more blindness." In spite of this truth, our story is predominantly one of aggression, power, and retribution. Significantly, it is a male narrative that operates on the principle that might is right. "Of arms and the man I sing," announced the poet Virgil, over two thousand years ago in the *Aeneid,* an epic that celebrated the glory of Rome at its zenith of power by recalling its founding myth.

Arms during the Graeco-Roman era were primitive indeed, compared to the means of destruction at hand today. Combat then was largely a matter of man-to-man engagement from chariots with supporting lines of infantry and archers. In the *Iliad,* another great epic with war as its subject, Homer describes the brutality and indignity of war in his time:

> Patroclus went up to him [Thestor] and drove a spear into his right jaw; he thus hooked him by the teeth and the spear pulled him over the rim of his car. As one who sits at the end of some jutting rock and draws a strong fish out of the sea with a hook and

> line—even so with his spear did he pull Thestor all gaping from his chariot; he threw him down on his face and he died while falling.

We have come a long way from the early Greek style of battle which, ugly and violent as it was, remained a confined and personal encounter between warriors. Obviously, the vast and impersonal devastation of modern nuclear warfare could never be conveyed via the image of a fish dangling on someone's hook.

It is only in the twentieth century that we have moved from war as a personal engagement of soldiers in battle to the wholesale, inhumane slaughter of innocent victims by the release of man-made bombs from the air. The aggressors do not even see that they are killing human beings. Their job is to hit targets. With the advent of the most destructive bombs of all time, the unbridled exercise of masculine power is no longer feasible, for it is far too sweeping and detached from the full human consequences of its aggression. We all stand endangered.

Peace, however, is not to be achieved by simply wanting it. Albert Einstein understood only too well the crucial and daunting challenge before us when he warned:

> The release of atomic energy has so changed every thing that our former ways of thinking have been rendered obsolete. We therefore face catastrophe unheard of in former times. *If mankind is to survive, then we need a completely new way of thinking.** (Italics mine.)

In the film *Matter of Heart: The Life of Carl Jung,* Marie Von Franz, when asked about Jung's last prophetic vision, clenches her hands and a look of acute distress crosses her face. Her voice tightens as she expresses her *angst* at the thought of life on this earth ending. As this wise old lady points out, there is no evidence of conscious life anywhere else in the galaxy. Millions of years have resulted in the development of conscious being that can be extinguished now in an instant—gone forever, like the dinosaurs before us. Madame Von Franz prays for a miracle.

Time is running out, but there is still hope for that miracle. If humankind is to

*Quoted by Georg Picht in Georg Picht and Wolfgang Huber, *Was heist Friedensforschung?* [What is Peace Research?] (Stuttgart: Ernst Klett Verlag: Kosel Verlag, 1971).

survive, we are faced with the challenge of a radical change in consciousness—one that involves the elevation of the feminine principle to balance the currently rampant masculine. Einstein was right: we do need a "completely new way of thinking." That new way requires that we think with our hearts as well as with our minds.

Helene Lange throughout her life insisted that the dissimilarity of the sexes must be emphasized in order that the feminine nature be freely developed and properly formed. Only then might this nature achieve its own cultural fulfillment, an achievement indeed necessary in our time as a suitable compensation for the obvious defects of our masculine Western culture; then feminine nature might be capable of authentic human formation and an activity of helping love.

Edith Stein, *Essays on Woman*

Chapter Three

Life Is a Balancing Act

Stressing the importance of environmental conditioning, Sigmund Freud nevertheless viewed biology as destiny. His aim was to restore human beings to an awareness of their natural roots by making them aware of their instinctual nature. Although the founder of classical psychoanalysis betrayed his ignorance of feminine psychology in his query, “What does a woman want?” he was, at least, open to the obvious facts of nature, which point to a profound dissimilarity of the sexes.

In the past, the biological and accompanying psychological differences between men and women were as plain as the breasts on a woman’s chest. Indeed, the traditional roles assigned to the sexes rested on these differences. Women, as nurturers, tended the domestic sphere of life while men, as providers and protectors of their families, challenged the outside world. Not only was sexual polarity accepted as the one invariant in all civilizations, but the sexual complementary relationship was unquestioningly seen as the very bedrock of the life process. Men and women, different as they were, needed each other for completion, survival, and procreation. Without the contribution of both sexes, life obviously could not go on.

Ancient religions and philosophies recognized that human polarity and human mating are aspects of an antithesis at the heart of things. For example, the ancient religion of Taoism, which is based essentially on nature, clearly expresses the idea that natural and historical events are influenced primarily by two principles: *Yin* and *Yang*. The feminine *Yin* is calm, dark, receptive, and the masculine *Yang* is active, light and generative. The Tao, a higher life principle of oneness equivalent to God, safeguards the reciprocal movement between the two.

In our dark, unbalanced age, the acceleration of technology, inspired by the masculine impulse, has led to a staggering degree of human arrogance along with a corresponding blindness to nature and her laws. Certainly, we have moved a long way from our natural roots. The cultural insanity, which has developed as a result of our era's imbalance and sexual confusion, has been vividly exemplified by the universal crazed enthusiasm of teenagers and young adults for pop singer Michael Jackson, who served for many years as a role model for his admirers. Naturally black, Jackson mysteriously emerged with bleached white skin, a high, feminine speaking voice, seductive long eyelashes and a pretty nose crafted by plastic surgery. As he masturbated and gyrated across the stage to an insistent, primitive musical beat, any mature adult had to wonder what his screaming audience saw in this obviously sick performer of indeterminate sex. In the past, Jackson probably would have been "put away" for the protection of socicty.

Sexual confusion, in itself, is not surprising in our twentieth century since, for the first time in history, there is a trend of thought that denies the biological determination of sexual identity and consequent sexual differences. The modern erroneous myth of essential sameness of female and male (before the influence of culture) circulates *holus bolus*. One of the early advocates of this view, Margaret Mead, in the fifties, concluded that the traditional roles of men and women depended largely on early conditioning as children. From Mead's point of view, the specific role of reproduction apart, sexual difference is a product of social and cultural institutions.

The tendency to gloss over sexual differences showed up in female thinkers before Mead. In the nineteenth century, author George Sand, writing to Flaubert, observed the tendency to overestimate disparities on the basis of anatomical differences. It is interesting to note that Sand, after many years of donning a male pseudonym along with masculine garb and privileges, returned to an enhanced femininity later in life. In her declining years, she recognized her family as her most important achievement.

Nowadays, the feminist claim to sexual equality has led to the notion that equality equals sameness. Profound thinkers such as Karl Stern recognize that the roots of this modern myth are complex. But it does not take a genius to know that the main root is the fact that women, down through the ages, not only have been mistreated socially and legally, but have been unappreciated and uncherished in their natural biological role as caregivers and nurturers. In spite of lip service to the contrary, currently there is still no gut level recognition of the value of the feminine in this regard. The observation in a local newspaper of a young mother, who gave up stimulating work on a Ph.D. in history because her children came first, is illustrative:

> . . . I think we still need to work on the attitude of some men toward the work women do in the house. We have to convince them that this is like a job. You put in long hours, it's hard work, and you don't get any vacations.*

This woman understates the issue when she refers to "some men" in need of a change of attitude toward the feminine domestic contribution. Men, though often supportive, nevertheless take these gifts quite for granted and have always done so. Since it is male accomplishment that society adulates, is it any wonder that many

*Ottawa Citizen, Sunday, 3 January 1994, Al.

women wish to share the male's place in the sun? They too would like to be valued. One cannot underestimate the importance of self-esteem. It is easy to see that the belief in the myth of sexual sameness offers a comforting illusion for many women in our male-oriented culture.

In *The Flight From Woman,* Karl Stern mentions the influence of the Cartesian view of the nature of the human being as another factor that influences the illusory myth of sexual similarity:

> The idea that anatomical differences are nothing but a matter of accidental implements of the body, interchangeable, as it were, is a touch of Cartesianism—something that imperceptibly creeps into many of our modern views of people and the world. (14)

Cartesianism, which originated with Descartes who verified his existence with the statement, "I think, therefore I am," tends to split the rational element of experience from the natural intuitive and prioritizes it. Stern notes that any basic truths about life that we derive from our observations of nature are now "suspect of magical thinking, and held to be open to correction by scientific inquiry." To the great impoverishment of humanity, natural truths that were held to be self-evident in the past are consigned to what is now thought of as the garbage dump of superstition. With all due consideration, it is rather astonishing that visible sexual differences and polarity, once so obvious to our ancestors, have to be proven scientifically today in order to achieve credibility.

Recently, in response to a survey claiming that high school girls showed diminished self-esteem compared to boys, an editor of a popular magazine asked, "Is the fact that girls' lives take a different turn from boys' a matter of nurture or nature?" The answer, of course, is both. It is psychological and common-sensical truth that heredity (biology) and environment are constantly interacting. There is no way of separating the two, much as we might like to try. The way in which a woman's or man's environment impacts on hereditary instinctual disposition affects identity.

Stern offers the act of sexual union as the basic example and paradigm of overall sexual distinction and function:

> The sex organs and the sex cells manifest a polarity and complementariness in morphology and in function. In the act of sexual union the male organ is convex and penetrating and the female organ is concave and receptive; the spermatozoon is torpedo-shaped and "attacks" and the ovum is a sphere "awaiting" penetration. That this polarity and complementariness should not be confined to the physical but also be reflected in the character of man and woman is a view as old as history. (9)

Stern's example corresponds with the masculine and feminine principles as seen by Taoism and Jungian psychology. The masculine is seen as energizing while the feminine is receptive. Though obviously different, both are necessary for the creation of life and are of equal value.

The feminine principle, which is one of receiving, keeping and nurturing, is part and parcel of the woman's specific form of creativeness—motherhood. The four week cycle of ovulation accompanied by menstruation, the nine months of gestation in pregnancy, and the act of childbirth tie women deeply to nature in a way that no man can easily understand. Every woman who has given birth knows only too well that in the final stage of labor her identity as an individual vanishes and she is taken over completely by the force of nature. Indeed, she becomes nature.

In contrast, the male embodies an aspect of life associated with the masculine principle that parallels the function of the sperm in relation to the ovum. While woman goes with nature, man attacks and penetrates it. Ever at the cutting edge, he digs up rocks and hacks down forests to make way for agriculture. He damns rivers in order to harness the power of water. Men, as chemists, break up molecules and rearrange atoms. Physicists have overcome the natural law of gravity, initially with the wheel and now with spaceships that penetrate the stratosphere. As Stern reminds us:

> Even in the realm of thought, in philosophy and in pure mathematics the "nature" of things is being "pierced" . . . Whether rocks are blasted to gain more soil or matter itself is destroyed (as in atomic fission) to gain more energy—man's activity is always in some way directed *against* nature. (23)

Clearly, the polarity of the sexes is based on sexual identity but not necessarily confined to it. According to Helene Deutsch, the masculine principle enables us all to master our relationship with reality and to solve problems rationally. This accounts for its being specifically named *Logos* by Jung. Significantly, men are recognized and valued for their singular inventiveness and toolmaking. Woman, according to Deutsch, "acts and reacts out of the dark, mysterious depths of the unconscious, i.e., effectively, intuitively, mysteriously" (150). In keeping with her biological maternal role, the feminine principle is called *Eros* by Jung who referred to the domain of the heart. Naturally, women are the experts in personal relationships and the realm of feeling. Clearly, the two principles do not preclude intelligence in women or feelings in men. They merely point to the specialties, the more natural modes, of the sexes.

The results of Carol Gilligan's survey, published in her ground-breaking work, *In A Different Voice* (1985), support the reality of sexual differences that are poles apart. Professor Gilligan studied a large group of students by asking them what they would do in a problematic situation involving the strict letter of the law versus the dictum of caring. She reports that women spoke of "the ongoing process of attachment which creates and sustains the human community." In contrast, for the men it is "the role of separation as it defines and empowers the self" (156). For women students in Gilligan's survey, the standard of moral judgment that informs their assessment of self is "the standard of relationship, the ethic of nurturance, responsibility and care" (159). The women measured their strengths "in the activity of attachment, ('giving to,' 'helping out,' 'being kind,' 'not hurting')." It is interesting that these highly successful and achieving women did not mention their academic and professional distinction when describing themselves. Gilligan cites another author, David C. McClelland, who reports that "while men represent powerful activity as assertion and aggression, women in contrast portray acts of nurturance as acts of strength" (167). The males in Gilligan's study were focused on self-empowerment and individual achievement. Great ideas or distinctive activity determined the way they measured themselves and their success in the world.

Following Gilligan's work, Deborah Tannen examined sexual differences in the area of linguistics. She discovered that men and women put language to disparate and conflicting uses. For women, the purpose of a conversation is to explore cooperative solutions to common problems. Sharing their feelings and experiences, they use language to enhance intimacy. The language of men focuses primarily on status. Independence is key in a hierarchical, competitive approach that strives for dominance. As Tannen points out, "taking orders is a marker of lower status" for men (26).

Significantly, Tannen notes that customarily "the male is seen as normative, the female as departing from the norm." In fact, she found that for many, the idea of gender differences in communication is acceptable as long as the woman is supposed to change (15). In addition, we might remind the reader that our culture labels feminine communication as "small talk."

Along with scholarly research on the subject of gender differences, television is a valuable indicator of current interests and offers corroboration in terms of program choices by men and women. Women watch "talk shows," which deal with problematic family and romantic relationships. The "soaps" also appeal to women, who avidly follow programs such as *The Bold and the Beautiful* and *The Young and the Restless,* continuing dramas about troubled relationships and the disappointments of love. Like dreams and literature, these programs reflect contemporary personal problems.

Men, on the other hand, are not intrigued by *eros* and relationships. Instead, they tune into aggressive action shows. Cowboys, gangsters, detectives, and lawyers in adversarial roles, verbally gunning down their victims, rivet the male imagination. Programs of the past, such as *Jake and the Fatman* and *McIvor,* portrayed varying degrees of violence in the good hero's quest to overcome evil. Pistol shootings, fistfights, and stabbings were condoned, even glorified, as long as they were used, simplistically, on the side of good. Moreover, there was no Mrs. Jake, Mrs. Fatman, or Mrs. McIvor in sight and the odd romance was a rare thing indeed. Let us not forget that Perry Mason, the lawyer esteemed for his brilliant, single-minded ability to ferret out and finish off the murderer, remained a bachelor to the end of his lengthy TV career. Good old Della, Mason's loyal secretary and girl Friday, steadfastly served her boss without imposing any emotional demands.

The persistence of the male preoccupation with aggression *to the exclusion of any tender feelings,* is a direct result of our long and bloody history of war. An inevitable outcome of the singularly masculine mode of attacking problems rather than discussing them and relating to the people involved, war has impaired the humane development of men, who are, in a sense, victims of a culture which perpetuates the masculine mode. From the moment that the little boy toddles off from his mother's skirt, he is taught by society to be a brave little soldier. Although some men cry more easily today, generally the young male who cries or exhibits any kind of meek behavior in public still does so at the risk of being labeled a "sissy" by his parents and peers.

In order to be prepared for combat at any time (war is at the very root of our culture), males are socially conditioned, albeit unconsciously, to be unemotional, competitive, successful, self-centered "top dogs." It is a win or lose world from their perspective and one does not win a war with normal access to the tender, caring feelings required for favorable human relationships. After all, how could anyone care about and kill his or her fellow man at the same time? Interestingly enough, the rather obvious but previously glossed over reality of social warrior conditioning has finally begun to reach popular attention. Therapists Diane Dunaway and Jonathan Kramer have informed readers in *Why Men Don't Get Enough Sex and Women Don't Get Enough Love* (1990) that while woman's energy is naturally channelled into "nurturing spirit," man's takes the form of "warrior spirit." Hence, the longstanding problem of the male's difficulty in expressing loving feelings to his mate.

Sadly for most men and women, the ways of war actually pervade the masculine approach to love. Men "conquer" their women. Women are "ravished" or "taken" by men. Currently, the violent rape of women (a timelessly common occurrence in war-torn countries) has been widely reported as a social problem of grave concern. South American writer Gabriel García Márquez provides an excellent example of warrior lovemaking in his 1988 bestseller, *Love in the Time of Cholera.* Longing for the great passion of his life, Fermina Daza, over a period of many years, the novel's hero, Florentino Ariza, finally beds his woman. He is impotent, or as García Márquez puts it, "unarmed."

But Florentino is not down for long. The next time, the author tells us, "His guard was up, and she [Fermina] realized that he did not expose his weapon by accident, but displayed it as if it were a war trophy in order to give him courage" (340). Needless to say, Florentino's "weapon" is not a gun or a knife, but a weapon for making love—his penis. The novel then describes a sexual onslaught that does not give Fermina time to remove her nightgown. Of course, the experience leaves her feeling desolate.

Largely directed as it is to the conquering of nature, the single-minded masculine approach has been extremely beneficial to the human species in terms of science and technology. As inventive toolmakers, men have brought us great ease, comfort, and longevity. With the flick of a switch, we have heat in unbearably cold winters and air-conditioning during torrid summers. Domestic work has been greatly facilitated with the invention of electricity and all the marvelous machines that followed. We now communicate more easily, frequently, and universally via telephone, fax machines, and Internet-connected computers. We travel extraordinarily long distances comfortably and quickly.

The list of benefits goes on and on. Not to be overlooked is the area of medicine with its life-saving miracles.

Technology has also delivered the means by which the entire human species can be blasted out of existence. Unfortunately, emotional development has not kept pace with the refinements and advances of man's genius for toolmaking. In terms of survival at this point in our history, the lack of personal understanding in men and their inability to relate empathetically to others is a serious impediment. While the masculine principle advances inexorably with increasingly sophisticated and, by now, redundant technology, few stop to consider that twentieth-century mechanical man and his culture are in jeopardy.

With nothing but more and better machines ahead of us, we are now at a critical stage wherein the unbridled masculine principle has almost extinguished the devalued feminine. Science and technology are revered by our culture rather than nurturance and life. War, though currently not as glorified as in the past, is still waged by male leaders who have not the slightest inkling of effective ways to promote peaceful relations; and the feminine principle of empathic, caring relationship (*eros*) is out in the cold.

Clearly, the problem is one of imbalance, individually and globally. There is absolute truth in the proverbial statement that life is a balancing act. In fact, when we observe that someone is not psychologically healthy, we call that person "unbalanced," a term we use all the time when describing emotional problems of various kinds. Individual and global balance can be meaningful only when we realize the basic truth expressed in Taoism: the prime element in the universal order involves *the interaction* of the opposites, the most important of which are *Yin and Yang*. According to the Tao, one must balance the other for optimal benefit to humankind. *Yin,* the feminine principle, is nutritive, warm and healing. A condition of aridity and sterility in society will set in if that society overvalues the *Yang,* or rational function. This is precisely what has occurred in contemporary civilization, as T.S. Eliot's *The Wasteland* makes abundantly clear. We now have gone far beyond even the condition portrayed in Eliot's spiritless neurotic characters. Today, we have pervasive danger throughout the world in the form of violence in the streets, continuous war between nations and the hovering threat of global extinction by nuclear holocaust.

William Phipps, a student of Christian history, quotes statements from the *Tao Te Ching* (the Taoist bible), which illustrate the need for the feminine to balance the masculine:

> In the *Tao Te Ching* these sentiments are expressed: He who knows the masculine but keeps the feminine . . . dwells in constant virtue. Grass and trees are supple and delicate when living but hard and stiff when they die, even so the hard and strong are comrades of death while the soft and tender are comrades of life. (74)

Such gems of wisdom can serve as valuable reminders to men, as well as to some women in our own culture who are prepared to disavow their femininity as a result of its devaluation.

Because the masculine principle is so highly valued, or, to put it more accurately, so over-valued, many women understandably are attracted to the traditionally male domain. Two world wars, of course, initiated the process whereby women can now work with their male peers and advance to powerful executive positions. There is always the danger, however, that women executives can place their employees in difficult and unpleasant situations if they assume predominantly masculine characteristics that lack caring, such as toughness, harshness, cruelty, and dictatorship. Emma Jung, wife of Carl Gustav and a physician and therapist in her own right, describes such women in her two essays, *Animus and Anima:*

> . . . there are those . . . in whom masculine behavior has overrun and suppressed the feminine principle. These are the over-energetic, ruthless, brutal, men-women, the Xantippes who are not only active but aggressive. (4)

Referring to these women as caricatures of men, Emma Jung explains this kind of masculine behavior in a woman as a response to society's elevation of the masculine principle to the exclusion of the feminine. As a culture, we pay lip service to the equality of women, but no one understands, at a gut level, the real meaning and value of the feminine principle. This will be fully discussed in the next chapter. In spite of the focus on women brought about by the feminist movement, Madame Jung points to reality:

> An American woman physician of wide experience has told me that all her women patients suffer from a depreciation of their own sex, and that with all of them she has to drive home the necessity of giving the feminine its due value. (24)

She adds: "On the other hand, there are extremely few men who undervalue their own sex." Emma Jung's essays were published in 1957 and she died shortly thereafter. One wonders what her thoughts might have been had she lived to see women as boxers, wrestlers and soldiers in combat.

Modern women, indeed, have been given much greater freedom than ever before, along with wide access to the previously male sphere of activity. There is, however, a real danger that the pendulum could swing the opposite way if hardened, unbalanced women push their luck too far. Margaret Atwood's futuristic novel, *The Handmaid's Tale,* envisions this possibility in the chilling scenario of a society in which women are enslaved with no voice whatsoever.

Still, in spite of the strong trend toward masculinization, there are women who have succeeded in previously masculine careers without losing their essential feminine identity. Such a woman, highly trained and experienced in business, was recently brought in to head a newly-formed company. Extremely attractive and feminine in appearance, this woman, who also has a unique level of competence and achievement, leads effectively. She combines firmness with the ability to give direction and sets up programs that make sense in particular situations. But she is an exceptional leader, in fact, superior to her male counterparts, because she also has a heart and relational skills. As a result, this executive is capable of listening to her employees and reflecting back the essential gist of what is being said to her. She tunes in, instead of riding roughshod over those reporting to her. Needless to say, all members of her staff love and respect her. Encouraged by her understanding, receptive attitude, they respond with their best efforts. It should be mentioned that the growth of the company, attributed specifically to her leadership, has been spectacular. Having met women of this calibre, Emma Jung confirms that their integrated personalities are for the best:

> But there are also women in whom this aspect of masculinity is already harmoniously coordinated with the feminine principle and lending it effective aid. These are the active, energetic, brave and forceful women. (4)

Edith Stein, early feminist, philosopher and Carmelite nun who wrote in the thirties, realized the importance of a balanced femininity. Stein clarified the innate essence of womanhood as the maternal, nurturing capacity and emphasized the important, positive influence of this mode in the family and in the working world at large. "Woman's attitude," Stein observed, "is generally a personal one and conducive to well-being in others" (Morin 191).

The lives of balanced women (like the executive we have discussed) illustrate the benefits that can accrue from harmonizing the masculine and feminine principles. If this kind of integration can take place within a human being, it is perhaps not too far-fetched to hope for the extension of *Yin/Yang* harmony in men and women on a global scale. This could change the entire pattern of human behavior and provide a way out of the constant human dilemma of inevitable clashes between people of different ideologies. Indeed, we might find a way to dispense with the futile and now imminently catastrophic "solution" of war. As Emma Jung points out:

> In our time, when such threatening forces of cleavage are at work, splitting peoples, individuals and atoms, it is doubly necessary that those which unite and hold together should become effective; for life is founded on the harmonious interplay of masculine and feminine forces, within the individual human being as well as without. Bringing these opposites into union is one of the most important tasks of present-day psychotherapy. (87)

The life stream can be compared to the energy of electricity. What we refer to as positive and negative charges are required for electricity. We equate the positive charge in life with the masculine principle and the negative charge with the feminine. The term "negative," of course, has undesirable connotations as something "less than," unconstructive, or with less potential. This is precisely the way our culture views the feminine principle. We fail to realize that both positive and negative charges—masculine and feminine—though very different, are equally vital to wholesomely balance the energy of life. Today, in fact, when the masculine is so dangerously heavy and pervasive, balance can only be achieved through a conscious recognition of the true value of the feminine mode. The all-but-eclipsed feminine must become the positive element.

Certain maladies of modern culture such as the dehumanization of the person, fragmentation, and the one-sided development of certain faculties leading to the atrophy of others may be cured through recourse to the intrinsic value of woman.

Edith Stein, *Essays on Woman*

Chapter Four

The Hand That Rocks the Cradle

Recently, a friend reminisced about her late father, a military officer: "That man certainly came to life during a war. He believed fervently that wars were needed to stimulate and renew bored, complacent societies." A large part of this soldier's excitement may have revolved around the reinforcement of his heroic self-image. In times of crisis, soldiers become our knights in shining armor, and rightly so since they risk their lives in order to protect us. In fact, our militia offers us a sense of security without which we would feel uncomfortably vulnerable.

We overlook, however, the cold hard reality that soldiers are trained killers and that war involves socially sanctioned murder. Men who think they are in the right kill men who are equally righteous. More often than not, each side sees itself as defending its homeland against the enemy. Meanwhile, innocent women and children die in this brutal and senseless endeavor.

Appalled when singular acts of torture perpetrated by our own soldiers come to light, we self-righteously punish the culprits. Since we view these episodes as uncivilized, rare, and shocking, it might be suggested that our hearts have not responded to the agonizing deaths of our fellow creatures who suffered the torture of war in Hiroshima, Nagasaki, Vietnam, and the Persian Gulf. War, after all, is hardly civilized behavior.

The antidote to war is empathy, which is the very essence of the feminine principle. Empathy is the capacity of sharing another's feelings or ideas, of walking in another's shoes. A psychiatric dictionary defines empathy more explicitly: "Putting oneself into the psychological frame of reference of another, so that the other person's thinking, feeling, and acting are understood and, to some extent, predictable." We cannot torture or kill other human beings if we understand and identify with them. Such identification encourages compassion and enables us to care about our enemies as fellow sufferers. As the well-known comic strip character Pogo said, "We have seen the enemy and it is us." This kind of enlightened, heartfelt, and humane approach has never been considered by our political leaders and military people. The commonplace, traditionally non-empathetic response is exemplified by the attitude of many American soldiers who were encouraged to view the Vietnamese people as depersonalized, dehumanized "geeks" during the war in Vietnam.

We fail to realize that in detaching ourselves from others we cannot relate to them. We see them then as dehumanized objects which are to be destroyed if they bother us. This attitude is part and parcel of a completely mechanized, almost schizoid, way of perceiving the world. It is a splitting of self from others, so that they become inhuman foreign entities rather than people like ourselves. Basically, this is a matter that touches on mental health because, in fact, we become detached from ourselves when we fail to tune into our fellow human beings. In healthy human terms, we must be seen, each of us, as particles of the whole rather than entities unrelated to one another.

The murderous aggression of war is the end result of a process of detachment. It is like a form of insanity. Clearly, we have no difficulty in seeing murderers in our society as "sick" people. We fail, however, to treat them as such and rather tend to lock them up in a kind of concentration camp atmosphere, separated from the rest of us. We might learn a lot from these people if we would but understand the simple truth that "there, but for the grace of God, go I. " If we could see murderers in this light, we might view them as *people,* seriously afflicted with a terrible disease, and we could set about trying to treat them in a humane and empathic manner.

It is interesting to note that a TV "talk show" hostess recently experimented with the notion of walking in another's shoes in order to develop empathic rapport. Trying to resolve various relational conflicts, this innovative woman had antagonistic parties exchange roles for a day. Husbands and wives, a mother and her daughter, and an employer and his employee came to a true appreciation of each other and a feeling of camaraderie and mutual support ensued.

Empathy is a quality that has always been in short supply. It has all but disappeared in today's world of extremely detached technology, so-called rationalism and self-interest. Once so necessary to survival, detached rationalism and logic, the essence of the masculine principle, have outgrown their usefulness in our human evolution since we have now literally conquered the earth. Indeed, we are currently in the process of tackling outer space and there is even talk of conducting war from this sphere. We have gone past the point of necessity into a crisis of extremity for (as I keep repeating) we face the imminent spectre of total annihilation of all life on this planet. The truth discovered by the Orientals thousands of years ago bears repeating: in the interplay of opposites, any pole unchecked by its opposite will run riot to become a destructive force.

Feminine intelligence is intimately tied to caring love, which is certainly beyond reason. Ordinarily, we think of intelligence as the exercise of logic, reason. As we have acknowledged before, man's ability to think analytically has been a vital tool for the survival of the human species. In limiting intelligence, however, to the area of the head we overlook the wisdom of the heart, which involves an intuitive insight into the deeper, more meaningful aspects of life, and which is necessary for an appreciation of life in the broadest sense. The wisdom of the heart, *eros*, involves our capacity for feeling, for love in the highest sense. We severely limit our humanity and our ability to live as whole human beings when we devalue and thus fail to tune into our capacity for emotion. In doing so, we do not realize that the feeling function has an intelligence of its own, necessary now more than ever, for survival. Hitler was a very intelligent man, even brilliant in terms of cold, hard logic, but he was an emotional imbecile. The consequences of his type of "macho" intelligence speak for themselves—the wholesale slaughter of millions of innocents for the sake of an ideal of a purified Aryan race. The ability to reason logically, divorced from the heart, can be diabolical!

We need to arrive at a new concept of intelligence as a quality that enables us to survive as a species by going beyond mere survival to a full, caring appreciation of life. We cannot appreciate life in the fullest sense if we do not care about our fellow humans and if we do not feel loved ourselves. Love affirms and confirms our value as human beings.

Love is every woman's primary focus in life. Ortega y Gasset pays tribute to the beauty and celestial "irrationality" of the feminine approach versus the masculine:

> The more of a man one is, the more he is filled to the brim with rationality. Everything he does and achieves, he does and achieves for a reason, especially for a practical reason. A woman's love, that divine surrender of her ultra-inner being which the impassioned woman makes, is perhaps the only thing which is not achieved by reasoning. The core of the feminine mind, no matter how intelligent the woman may be, is occupied by an irrational power. If the male is the rational being, the woman is the irrational being.

To most, the word "irrational" has the negative implication of "foolish," or "stupid," even "crazy." There are many wise thinkers, however, who realize that the feminine irrational way has a profound value and logic of its own—that of the heart.

Empathy, which is an intuitive way of knowing, is central to genuine caring love for it is the bridge of human spiritual connections and real relationships. Without this quality, there is no love; individuals, though ostensibly joined, remain narcissistic islands driven by unrealistic projections. Empathy is also (as previously stated) the very essence of true femininity. Edith Stein describes this innate capacity of woman: "She has the special gift of making herself at home in the inner world of others" (178).

This connecting tendency leads naturally to the impulse to serve others. So, it is not surprising that women are effective in the area of sales, as well as in services such as medicine and teaching. Anyone who has been waited on by both saleswomen and salesmen can readily attest to the superior kind of attention offered by women. Undoubtedly, men do their best but they are usually handicapped by their inability to tune into the customers' needs. Ask a man about an item that you are shopping for and he is likely to say, while pointing in a general direction, "It's over there," or "If you don't see it on the shelf we don't have it." He might, however, give you important information about the product. A woman, on the other hand, gives you a special feeling that may be hard to describe because it is not rational. She gives you the feeling that she is really there for you; she absorbs your request and she cares. Carefully listening to your needs, a saleswoman will probably stay with you to assist with helpful suggestions. Of course, during difficult economic times, many stores are understaffed and we do not always receive such ideal help. We all know the experience of helpless frustration when we are denied easy access to this kind of service. Indeed, we feel so neglected that we are likely to walk out of the store. Occasionally, good fortune provides us with a man and woman working as a team (generally the store owners). This can be quite a treat: the man offers facts about the product and the woman jumps in with practical suggestions about personal suitability. In a way, the enterprise resembles a symphony with two distinct themes, together making a beautiful, harmonious piece of music. Left, however, with a choice between the sexes in most service areas, we might prefer the woman, who will try to tune into our needs and will graciously go out of her way to satisfy them.

Empathy is part of a woman's instinctual equipment. To the female of the human species falls the most important, yet least appreciated task of life—the nurturing and character formation of the future generation. Her empathic, soothing response to the frequently raging and helpless infant determines the child's basic sense of being valued, along with a sense of trust in the world, (i.e., the certainty that the world is a reliable place). The inarticulate, helpless infant depends on the mother's empathic ability to decipher and meet its needs.

Moreover, it is the mother who lays the groundwork for the degree of her offspring's empathic potential or lack of it. Heinz Kohut, the psychoanalyst known for his successful treatment of narcissistic personality disorders (particularly common to our era), discovered that many patients seeking psychotherapy suffer from a profound disturbance of self-esteem, the essence of which is a defect in the person's sense of inner cohesion and continuity or to put it another way, an insufficient consolidation of the self. Kohut's patients were able to achieve wholeness by reliving an empathetically improved mother relationship in the transference situation. Kohut declares, "The potential for the acquisition of a special talent for empathic perception . . . as well as the propensity for the enjoyment of exercising this psychological function is largely acquired early in life" (277). Clearly, the child who is reared by an empathic mother will tune into others more naturally.

Indeed, the mother's influence on the course of her child's life is far stronger than most of us like to acknowledge. As the nineteenth-century poet William Ross Wallace wrote in his poem, *The Hand That Rules the World:* "The hand that rocks the cradle is/ The hand that rules the world" (Stanza 1) . Although Wallace' s statement has assumed the status of a proverb, few in our culture recognize the important truth embodied in this insight. Operating on the masculine principle, we refuse to face the fact that the job of child-rearing is more important than the business of the world. Worse, still, we ignore the obvious importance of the mother in this essential task.

In his analysis of the roots of instinctual development Freud, the founder of depth psychology, considered the paternal influence as pivotal in the child's life. From his point of view, the oedipal crisis in childhood profoundly influenced adult neuroses. Freud's bias, at that time, was natural enough since the voices of his female colleagues had not yet been heard.

With the emergence of women, analysts such as Helene Deutsch, Karen Horney, Anna Freud and, in particular, Melanie Klein, the fundamental importance of the mother-infant relationship received the recognition it so richly deserved. As Hanna Segal says, "Freud acquainted us with the child in the adult, and Klein with the infant in the child" (Sayers 254).

Klein broadened psychoanalysis and changed its direction from concern with the father's repressive influence on the child's instincts to a primary emphasis on the instincts as related to the maternal figure. Janet Sayers summarizes Klein's contribution in *Mothering Psychoanalysis:*

> While Anna Freud shunned mothering, Melanie Klein embraced it both for good and for ill. She thereby brought about a revolution in psychoanalysis, from concern with patriarchal taming of the child's "lawless instincts" . . . to an understanding of instincts as always related to others, in the first place to the mother as loved and hated. Increasingly, she demonstrated these relations—not the instincts shorn of relations to others—to constitute the stuff of mental life. (205)

Many men, following Klein's shift in direction, have made significant contributions which flesh out the maternal influence on child development.

Admitting that he was limited as a man, Freud ultimately acknowledged the feminine contribution to depth analysis:

> Everything in the sphere of this first attachment to the mother seemed to me so difficult to grasp in analysis—so grey with age and shadowy and almost impossible to revivify—that it was as if it had succumbed to an especially inexorable repression. But perhaps I gained this impression because the women who were in analysis with me were able to cling to the very attachment to the father in which they had taken refuge from the early phase that was in question. It does indeed appear that women analysts . . . have been able to perceive these facts more easily and clearly because they were helped in dealing with those under their treatment by the transference to a suitable mother-substitute. (Sayers, epigraph)

Freud's statement does suggest the need for masculine and feminine views in the search for truth.

Benefiting from the discoveries in child development by both women and men since Freud's time, the European-born Canadian psychiatrist Karl Stern shows an almost poetic understanding of the paramount mother-child relationship. He describes the intimate rapport between mother and infant as a *participation mystique:*

> There exists a *participation mystique,* a psychic flow from child to mother and from mother to child. (18)

Stern elaborates:

> There exists a deeply *knowing* relationship between child and mother—a mode of knowledge which *precedes* the advent of reason and, in a sense, *transcends* it. (32)

Eros is at the center of this formative bond.

As Stern explains, the woman as mother is the first person with whom we are in steady contact. Our existence begins with the most intimate union possible between two human beings, a union which shapes our entire fate. It involves a fusion wherein the child is first sheltered and nourished in the mother's womb, and that remarkable closeness and communication continues for a long time after birth. We all start our lives in utter helpless dependence on the mother (or her substitute) and continue in this state for a prolonged period. In fact, of all the species on earth, humankind is dependent on the mother for the longest span of life. Our experience of reliance on the maternal figure is even longer when we consider that time is sensed as moving very slowly when we are young. We are totally dependent on our care-giver for the first seven years of life, for we would starve if she did not feed us, and we would live in squalor and illness if we were not kept clean. After that period, we continue to rely on maternal care. But there is more to human nurturance than the physical. We all depend on our mothers for spiritual nourishment, love. We see ourselves in the eyes of our first lover. Ideally, the mother's instinctive, empathic, steady, protective identification with her infant's helpless condition and with its needs provides a sense of security; her maternal comforting, soothing and adoration gives the child the sense that he or she is important to her and, therefore, of value.

Above all, the mother's empathic response, which involves her mirroring of the infant, lays the groundwork for her offspring's feeling of reality and identity. In a compassionate analysis of the roots of the daughter Emily's neurosis and alienation in Tillie Olsen's short story, *I Stand Here Ironing,* Robert J. Kloss examines the nurturing deficiencies in Emily's early formative years. It is to Kloss's credit that he also recognizes the early deprivation in the mother's upbringing and, consequently, empathizes with her plight as a mother rather than judging her. Kloss links Emily's search for validation with inadequate empathic mirroring by the mother:

> . . . she has never had her own existence and separateness from her mother fully confirmed by adequate *mirroring,* the eyes of the mother that establishes the basic trust of consistency, continuity and sameness of care provided by that mother. Through this process, intimately linked to breast feeding and stimulation of the smile response, the infant makes mother, once an outer predictability, into an inner certainty, a sense that the world is a good place where one's needs are provided for. (84)

Obviously, there is no blame attached to the severely limited mother; one cannot give what one did not get. Kloss concludes that, ideally, in the eyes of the mother, "The infant finds confirmation of his own existence, the initial sense not of *who* I am, but *that* I am" (84).

Today, in our highly technologized world, one could possibly foresee the invention of a Robot Mom, with skin that would feel silkily human, programmed to respond to the cries of the infant for food, comfort and reassurance. There is no way, however, that a robot could tune into and reflect the child, nor could it possibly understand the reason for the child's distress and distinguish its various needs. Such involvement requires the living spirit of love, the mystery of which no technological genius will ever capture in a machine. One can surely agree with the value that Kloss assigns to adequate nurturing and his assessment of the damage of deprivation:

> Optimal mirroring therefore aids the child in consolidating his own identity because it enables him as a separate entity to realize the existence of a separate object out there, an "I" vs. a "not-I." On the other hand, poor mirroring—insufficient holding, smiling, gazing, nurturing—leads to deeply rooted conflicts. (84)

As damaging as a deficiency of maternal empathy can be, the loss of the mother at an early age can be even more traumatic for the child. René Spitz's research, depending largely on direct observations, proved that prolonged separation from the maternal figure during infancy causes emotional and intellectual defects beyond restoration. According to Spitz, the age between six months and eighteen months is the most critical period of bereavement. Infants who lose their mothers during this span go through an extreme reaction of mourning. In spite of the best conditions of child care and nutrition, they regress in their mental development, lose weight, and are overly susceptible to infections. Their facial expression and attitudes are strikingly similar to those of psychotically depressed adults (Stern 35).

In dwelling on the importance of the maternal role in child-rearing, it is not our intention to "lay a guilt trip" on women. The purpose, rather, is to drive home the point that the feminine principle, as embodied in the maternal nurturing role, is so powerfully decisive for the formation of character and mental health. The early drama between mother and child takes place before conscious reasoning stirs in the child and is more profoundly experienced than anything occurring later in life. This initial relationship also sets the basic imprint of how we view ourselves and the world around us. As Karl Stern points out, it "leaves traces at the rock-bottom of the human condition" and "sets a pattern for all stories to come in the individuals life" (19).

In order, however, for the woman's instinctive nurturing capacity—her empathic care—to flourish optimally, she must also be emotionally nourished. The woman is very needy in the maternal role and requires support, appreciation and encouragement. Her domestic task is additionally demanding since, traditionally, the woman has been constantly at the beck and call of her family. Truthfully, a woman's work in the home while raising children is sheer drudgery if it is not a labor of love. If she receives no appreciation and love, she is bound to feel like Cinderella stuck in the kitchen. If a beautiful flower is neglected, it will shrivel up and die; it requires water, light and proper soil. The same truth applies to the loving soul of the woman.

The feminine principle embodied in

the soul of woman has not been cared for in our culture. In human terms, this means that the woman has not been cherished for her arduous contribution to our lives. Rather, in her domestic/maternal role she has been taken for granted, ignored and too often abused. As Emma Jung declared in *Animus and Anima,* man "for centuries has exploited woman and misused her" (78). This mistreatment goes hand in hand with mankind's disregard for nature, for, again quoting Emma Jung (a woman ahead of her time), "The intellectual viewpoint dominant in an era of science and technology leads to utilizing and even exploiting nature, rather than honoring her" (87). There is no denying the fact that woman, because she gives birth and also because of her aura of mystery, is identified with nature.

Like it or not (and these days women, understandably, do not like it), nature intended woman as her handmaiden to serve the species. Instead, she has been treated like a slave. Finally, she has rebelled, as slaves will ultimately do. Many women today are turning away from this thankless role.

Ironically, the servants role, which is so vital to our existence on this earth, has never been appreciated. Looked down on as the lowliest, least prestigious "career choice," it is really the most important one. Humanity has always been ambivalent about the servant's position. On the one hand, service to one's fellow human beings is regarded as the highest virtue. Indeed, Christ exemplifies this ideal of every Christian's life. But, at the same time, this role is recognized as humble and powerless and few are willing to sacrifice feelings of power over their own fate, which submission to another requires. The Church itself demonstrates its ambivalence when it emphasizes, constantly, Christ's power in the miracles he performed. Power and love, however, are incompatible.

Conflicted though we may be over the issue, service to others is still a great virtue and a *necessity* in life. Where would we be without people to serve us? We would, in fact, be lost. We all need, want, and love to be served! Without this aspect of human behavior, we feel left out in the cold. Cut off from caring fellow creatures, we might as well be dead, for who could stand such alienation for any length of time? Surely, we have all experienced the momentary anxiety and frustration of hearing a dead, recorded voice on the telephone when we need to be served by a live human being, someone who actually listens to our personal requirements.

Mothers have been the greatest servants of all. Often prepared to sacrifice their lives for their children, down through history they have served their families. Women still love to serve others, knowing full well that to do so is an act of generosity that gives great pleasure to the giver as well. But that pleasure quickly disappears when the gift is ignored, taken for granted, or received with a superior "sour grapes" attitude. A friend, now divorced, reminisced about the random thoughts she often entertained during her marriage while standing at the kitchen sink washing the dinner dishes. Her husband was a dour fellow, much absorbed in his work, sports, and many hobbies. After serving a delicious dinner to her family, Janet would watch her husband disappear into the recreation room without so much as a word to her. Gritting her teeth, she would think, "Boy, if he only realized that I would stand on my head for him if he would just put his arm around me, give me a hug, or tell me that I'm a great cook."

Another example of ingratitude that comes to mind is the working relationship of Edith Stein and her mentor, the great philosopher Husserl. Edith gave up her own teaching career in order to be of service to this important thinker who, during World War I, was left without the customary male assistant. Husserl, a typical absent-minded professor who scribbled his thoughts and lectures on various bits of paper, required someone to put these notes into some kind of order. Studying the specific shorthand in which her boss set his ideas on paper, Edith painstakingly sorted, deciphered, transcribed and catalogued the monumental mess, bringing to light ideas of great significance. Husserl, however, paid no attention to the carefully organized body of work, but consistently set off on new developments of thought. Frustration was Edith's daily bread. Her careful attention and painstaking work went unnoticed and unappreciated. No doubt asking herself "What's it all in aid of?" she resigned her position about a year and a half later.

For the classic *pièce de resistance* among examples of neglect of the feminine contribution, we must consider Virginia Woolf's, *To the Lighthouse.* In the novel, concerning the marital drama of the Ramsays, Woolf sets up a contrast between masculine and feminine qualities, values and behavior. The cold, dry, sharp imagery associated with Mr. Ramsay, a philosophy professor ("Alpine peaks of abstract thought," "the fatal sterility of the male plunged itself, like a beak of brass, barren and bare"), stands next to the "delicious fecundity" and the constant nurturing activity of Mrs. Ramsay. Another image of the husband, "the arid, scimitar of the male, which smote mercilessly, again and again, demanding sympathy" (53) effectively conveys the man's totally self-absorbed, inconsiderate, excessive demand for attention and pity from his spouse. Mr. Ramsay, in fact, is a little boy with a bottomless pit consisting of a never ending need for nurturing and ego bolstering. So absorbed is he with his narcissistic requirements that he offers little, beyond critical correction, to his wife and family. Mrs. Ramsay, on the other hand, is busy from dawn to dusk doing for and giving to others. We see her in her domestic role, knitting a child's stocking; we see her as a mother, reading a story to her son James and comforting the younger children when they go to bed; we see her as a hostess, presiding at the table; and we see her as a wife, yielding to her demanding husband. She is, as we tend to say, "just" a mother, "just" a wife.

In her introduction to the 1992 World's Classics edition of the novel, Margaret Drabble recognizes the vital service provided by Mrs. Ramsay as the altruistic, loving, creative center of her family:

> . . . Mrs. Ramsay's creativity is of another order—and of what now, in this post-feminist age, may seem a peculiarly old-fashioned, womanly order. She is a creator of harmony, of beautiful moments, of memories. She charms and reconciles. She draws out the bores and cheers the downhearted and visits the sick. She comforts her children with fantasies and indulgences. (xxi-xxii)

As Drabble suggests, modern women are no longer willing to accept this sacrificial role. We might add that husbands like Mr. Ramsay are a large part of the reason for this tragic loss.

Unfortunately, no one seems to realize that the woman, in her demanding maternal role, requires nurturing as well, a fact that is glaringly obvious in the life of Mrs. Ramsay. No one stops to think of conditions that would be favorable to her comfort and growth. We find her, following one of the many sympathy sessions devoted to her mate, with "scarcely a shell of herself left for her to know herself by" because "all was so lavished and spent." Mr. Ramsay leaves this encounter "restored, renewed," but his wife "seemed to fold herself together, one petal closed in another, and the whole fabric fell in exhaustion upon itself" (54).

It comes as no surprise when this beautiful, untended flower, deprived of the water and light of empathic solicitude, dies suddenly and prematurely. We are informed of her death briefly and in brackets:

> [Mr. Ramsay stumbling along a passage stretched his arms out one dark morning, but, Mrs. Ramsay having died rather suddenly the night before, his arms, though stretched out, remained empty.] (175)

A lengthy, detailed description of the utter neglect and deterioration of the Ramsay summer home deprived of its homemaker, however, conveys the full impact of Mrs. Ramsay's demise. The place, quite literally, becomes uninhabitable. The family moves out and does not return for many years.

Mrs. Ramsay's death and the consequent decay of the summer home serve as a paradigm for the universal demise of the wounded feminine principle. The mother who nurtures full time has all but disappeared. As we have said before, two world wars, requiring women's input in the previously male working world, gave women a taste of freedom, economic independence and opportunities for socially-valued employment. Given society's lack of appreciation for the domestic nurturing role, it is only natural these days that healthy, ambitious women virtually have no alternative but to head for more rewarding positions. Most women, understandably loath to give up their newly won self-esteem, but wanting marriage and children, eventually carry a double burden of family and "outside" career. Unfortunately, with overburdened mothers who are unable or unwilling to "just" serve exclusively as the nurturing center of the home (a full-time job in itself), the family, which is the basic living cell of society, has gone awry. It no longer functions in a healthy way because it has lost its heart and hearth.

"Home is where the heart is," the old saying goes. But we no longer pay attention to words of wisdom from the past. The heart is the empathic, compassionate nurturing of the mother and we have lost sight of this vital element. We tend to think that survival is a matter of adequate food, housing and clothing. Certainly these things are essential but, by themselves, they are not enough to keep the human race going.

Surely the statement about the influence of the mother on each and every life bears repeating "The hand that rocks the cradle rules the world." Our fate is shaped from the beginning by a personal relationship with mother; the experiences that determine this destiny originate in a preconceptual and prelogical realm. Moreover, as adults we never lose the need for mothering in terms of contact with caring people. But the feminine in principle remains unacknowledged and, therefore, uncherished in our culture.

The symbol of mothering in the Judaeo-Christian religion which has informed our civilization is Mary. Down through the centuries, devotees have prayed to "Our Lady," but, until 1945, she had no official place in heaven. Carl Jung realized that the assumption of Mary into heaven, where at last she keeps company with her son, Jesus, and God, heralded a significant change in Catholic dogma. Hopefully, this symbolic event of Mary's elevation presages a future balance of masculine and feminine principles here on earth.

The qualities primarily associated with Mary are grace and mercy; both essentially go hand in hand with the capacity for empathy. One of the Rosary prayers addresses Mary, "Hail Mary, full of grace." In a theological context, grace means "unconstrained and undeserved divine favor or goodwill" and "God's loving mercy displayed to man for the salvation of his soul" (Webster). In other words, grace is unconditional love and Mary is filled with this wonderful life-affirming capacity. In everyday Catholic prayers, Mary is hailed as the "holy Queen, Mother of mercy." As children turn to their mother for comfort, so do believers appeal to Mary:

> Hail, holy Queen, Mother of mercy, our life, our sweetness, and our hope. To you we cry, poor banished children of Eve. To thee do we send up our sighs, mourning and weeping in this vale of tears. Turn then, most gracious advocate, thine eyes of mercy towards us. And after this our exile, show unto us the blessed Fruit of thy

womb, Jesus. 0h clement, 0h loving,
0h sweet Virgin Mary.

In a spiritually barren world so out of touch with nature and so unbalanced by masculine materialism and technology, this prayer poignantly expresses the need for the feminine as a source of sweetness, mercy and hope. In the final analysis are we not all, now more than ever, banished children in this mysterious "vale of tears" called life?

Mary's virginity suggests, essentially, an innocence that places her in the context of unscheming nature. There is no lust associated with her, no ulterior purpose of "hooking" a man. Femininity is closely identified, indeed, with Mother Nature. The rhythm of menstruation, pregnancy, the labor of birth, and the nurturing process remind the woman that she is part of the ebb and flow of nature. While the man asserts himself against nature in order to control and conquer it, the woman has no choice but to go with the flow.

Mercy (associated with Mary), the corollary of empathy, is part of the "feeling" world and cannot be legislated, controlled or forced. This simple truth is divinely expressed in Portia's well-known words to Shylock and the court in Shakespeare's *The Merchant of Venice*. Probably one of the most fallibly human of Bard's characters, Shylock is bent on receiving the pound of flesh promised to him in default of Antonio's debt. Ruled by the Old Testament principle of "an eye for an eye," Shylock represents every man from time immemorial to the present in his desire for justice: "Today I stand for judgment." How often have we seen the relatives of murder victims bitterly insist on the death penalty for a killer? Indeed, our entire legal system is based on the idea of punitive retribution. In her judicial capacity, Portia urges Shylock to "be merciful." Shylock, however, interprets her request as a command. Mired as he is in the masculine mode of control, he has no understanding of the concept of mercy. He responds: "On what compulsion must I? Tell me that" (iv, i, 183). Portia then explains that mercy transcends control:

> The quality of mercy is not strain' d,
> It droppeth as the gentle rain from heaven
> Upon the place beneath. It is twice blest:
> It blesseth him that gives and him that takes.
>
> It is an attribute of God himself,
> And earthly power doth then show likest God's
> When mercy seasons justice. (184-202)

It is significant that these words, which describe the nature and supreme value of mercy, are spoken by a woman. Portia does not present an either/or solution: justice (the masculine principle) needs to be tempered by mercy (the feminine principle). Still, mercy is of the highest order because it transcends the normal human mode: "It is an attribute of God himself."

War is a singularly merciless endeavor. Frequently masquerading under idealistic banners, it sanctions the slaughter of innocent people. At the present time with the technology available, war as the solution to power conflicts threatens the extinction of the entire human species.

Likewise, the disappearance of the feminine principle from the domestic scene invites the disintegration of society.

The abyss of error in which we live concerning women and our relations with them.

Leo Tolstoy, *The Kreutzer Sonata*

Man does not generally envisage relationships other than as power relations. He chases, approaches or seduces a woman to conquer her; the language he uses is revealing and sounds more like that of a sailor, hunter or warrior than of a lover.

Emmanuel Reynaud,
Holy Virility: The Social Construction of Masculinity

What a wondrous place this planet would be if man and woman, black and white, old and young could value and love each other not as objects, but as participants in the same cosmic journey.

June Singer, *Androgyny: Toward a New Theory of Sexuality*

Chapter Five

Slam, Bam—Thank You, Ma'am!

Some time ago, an eye-witness report on the intricacies of labor union negotiations appeared on television. It was a jolting experience to hear the dialogue of reputable pillars of the working community. A tough, abusive barrage of language exploded like rifle shots. Almost every sentence uttered by these illustrious leaders included the words "fuck" and "fucking:" "What the fuck are they up to?" "That isn't the fucking way to go;" "These fucking negotiations are taking too long;" "You were wrong to take that fucking action, Al;" "Let's send out for our fucking supper," and so on.

True, this unimaginative style of communication is hardly a novelty these days.

Since the publication of D.H. Lawrence's novel, *Lady Chatterly's Lover,* the "f-word" has invaded our language progressively in film, literature, and everyday conversation. It is particularly prevalent in the tough world of men. Apart from revealing an extremely impoverished vocabulary, the gratuitous use of this aggressive expletive highlights the masculine attitude toward the sexual expression of love. Certainly, there is no avoiding the obvious fact that the most abusive word in our language describes the act of sexual intercourse. The *Random House Dictionary* first defines the word "fuck" as "to have sexual intercourse," and then offers the more generalized slang use, "to treat unfairly."

Singularly courageous souls such as feminist Andrea Dworkin have exposed the commonly aggressive, unloving male approach to sex and its stultifying effects. We need to take an honest look at the cultural incentives to this dehumanizing state of affairs. At the root of the average man's inability to approach the most intimate aspect of adult human bonding in a tender, caring way is the unconscious cultural warrior conditioning he is exposed to from childhood. It is important to recognize that war is, and has always been, in the background when not in the foreground of our civilization. The "slam, bam—thank you, ma'am" treatment that many, if not most, women receive in their sexual relations with the opposite sex (excluding, perhaps, the still uncommitted pursuit of the courtship dance) is the central aspect of a universal flight from woman and feminine values lest "he-man" defenses collapse. As previously stated, the qualities so necessary for battle—physical strength, toughness, competitiveness, daredevil courage, and violence—leave little room for tender feelings. Warriors must be killers and so the world has never admired so-called "sissies" and "softies." Nevertheless, as long as we encourage men to be tough heroes rather than tender, empathic human beings, we will have inadequate lovers, crippled relationships between the sexes and, of course, war. Perhaps the hippies of the sixties were close to the truth when they admonished, "Make love, not war."

Unfortunately, as Andrea Dworkin points out in her ground-breaking book, *Intercourse,* most men do not really make love. With a rare honesty and directness, Dworkin analyzes the basic act of human procreation, which epitomizes the relationship between men and women. She asks whether sexual intercourse is an act of intimate communion or merely the socially sanctioned and celebrated exploitation of women. The fact that Dworkin uses the word "fuck" blatantly and repeatedly to describe male involvement in the sexual act pretty well confirms her conclusion: men fuck women rather than make love to them. Interestingly, the four-letter word itself has a harsh, punchy sound that connotes aggression, while the expression "make love" is soft, mellifluous and melting to the ear.

Dworkin opens *Intercourse* with examples of the sexual habits of two great artists, Gustav Mahler and Count Leo Tolstoy. About the genius who gave the world such hauntingly beautiful music, she writes: "Usually, when Gustav wanted intercourse, he waited until Alma [his wife] was asleep, or pretended to be; then he would begin his lovemaking" (3). Obviously, the use of the word "lovemaking" is meant to be ironic and Dworkin, indeed, reports subsequently that the composer did no more than "fuck" his wife. Mahler's surreptitious, inconsiderate mode of self-gratification represents a complete denial of his wife's living response and involvement. It comes as no surprise to find that Dworkin's research into Alma Mahler's life reveals a beautiful, sensitive woman who was "tired, alienated and unhappy in her marriage" and who felt that she was married to a stranger (3).

The relationship between Leo Tolstoy and his wife, Sophie, was also problematic. Dworkin outlines the central marital dilemma from Sophie's point of view:

> The woman had an argument; her husband should love her as a human being, not only use her as an object when he wanted to fuck her. The woman had an analysis: her husband was selfish to a rare and horrifying degree, also a hypocrite; people were real to him only insofar as they affected him personally; she was real to him only when and because he wanted physical love; he became cold when he was sexually sated and indifferent to her. (5)

Once again we get the picture of a man who was unable to accept and embrace his woman in a caring way.

Dworkin points out that Sophie Tolstoy has been the butt of most biographers' blame. She illustrates:

> The author of *Tolstoy and Gandhi, Men of Peace,* for instance, blamed her for "a continual denial of Tolstoy's beliefs and an irritable and sometimes hysterical ridicule," also "moral triviality" and "inconsistency and brute egotism." (5)

One has to realize that Martin Green, the author of *Tolstoy and Gandhi,* views the marriage from a particularly masculine point of view. Indeed, who was denying whom? Moreover, it hardly seems likely that the wife, rather than the husband, would have had the characteristic of "brute egotism." It is true, however, that most biographers have seen Sophie as an hysterical, grasping, and difficult wife. If this were so, who could blame the woman since she had such a difficult husband? Blaming the woman for things that go wrong is part of a tradition that goes back to the Biblical story of Adam and Eve. An old movie (*Gilda*), which featured actress Rita Hayworth singing "Put the blame on Mame, boys," comes readily to mind.

Apparently, Sophie Tolstoy anticipated biographic misconceptions and prejudice in favor of her husband:

> She would not have been surprised. "And his biographers," she wrote in

> 1895, "will tell of how he helped the laborers to carry buckets of water, but no one will ever know that he never gave his wife a rest and never—in all these thirty-two years—gave his child a drink of water or spent five minutes by his bedside to give me a chance to rest a little, to sleep, or to go out for a walk or even just to recover from all my labors." (Dworkin 5)

Sophie's labors were truly oppressive. According to Dworkin, she had thirteen children, six of whom died of difficult and painful illnesses such as meningitis and croup. She developed puerperal fever and other female infections, which included inflamed breasts. A dutiful and interested wife, Sophie transcribed all of her husband's books and diaries except for a short period when Tolstoy, feuding with his wife, handed the job to his adult daughters in order to exclude her. The Countess educated the children and managed her husband's estates, money, and copyrights from 1883. She fed and nurtured the children while, simultaneously, looking after the publication of his books, sometimes pleading with the state censor for permission to publish them (6).

In spite of such a back-breaking burden, Sophie continued to service her husband sexually until late in the marriage when she finally moved out of the bedroom she shared with the Count. At this point, enough was enough and Sophie wanted no more intercourse. This move, however, did not deter Tolstoy who remained indifferent to his wife's needs and feelings:

> It was not until 3 July 1897, that she moved out of the marital bedroom, not wanting to have intercourse anymore, but Tolstoy continued to fuck her when he wanted and to ignore her the rest of the time. She hated "his coldness, his terrible coldness"—his indifference to her after intercourse which changed only when he wanted intercourse again. (Dworkin 6)

Following Tolstoy's death, which occurred at age eighty-two, shortly after he left her, Sophie wrote in her diary that physical love never "meant an emotional game to me, but always something very much akin to suffering" (Dworkin 37). In her 1891 diary, she wrote that all she wanted while her husband lived was "warm, gentle affection." Instead, she endured "these outbursts of passion always followed by long periods of coldness" (Dworkin 90).

Should the reader be inclined to see Mahler's and Tolstoy's alienated and alienating sexual treatment of their wives as unique and attributable to neurotic genius, be assured that many disclosures from women in similar situations have reached the ears of psychotherapists. One disillusioned woman, reportedly, complained bitterly about being awakened many a night by her husband's selfish sexual advances. This lusty fellow never stopped to consider that his exhausted wife might require an unbroken night of sleep after an emotionally and physically draining day of caring for their four energetic young children. Other women have expressed their bewilderment over husbands who insult or shout at them during the day and expect sexual proximity at night. Still others cannot understand how their husbands can expect sex at the end of a day void of any communication—not a word, kind or otherwise—from the man. A counselor practicing in Los Angeles recalled hearing an ardent feminist proclaim to a group of women: "When I finally left my husband after twenty years of marriage, I ended a role that combined slavery with prostitution!"

The disappointment of women in their sexual relationships with men is beginning to surface in contemporary fiction, which reflects the realities of everyday life. One of the focal points in Carol Shield's Pulitzer Prize winning novel, *The Stone Diaries,* is the selfish, unfeeling sexual performance of the male. Interestingly enough, the image of cold, hard, inanimate stone, which runs through the novel, underscores the absence of human warmth portrayed. The title, which evokes a harsh ambience even before the book is opened, sets the tone of the lives of Mercy Stone Cuyler and her daughter Daisy Goodwill. Turning the pages, the reader discovers that Daisy is born in the town of Stonewall. Her mother Mercy has spent her childhood and adolescence in the Stonewall Orphans Home where she shared the surname "Stone" with the other orphans, given over to the institution's care as infants by their unmarried mothers (29). The common surname is particularly apt since these institutionalized children were deprived of maternal love, the warm nurturing bond that validates and affirms the infant. Instead, they were raised in a stony institution. Mercy moves from the orphanage directly into a marriage to Cuyler Goodwill who, along with other men in the area, works in the Stonewall Quarry, aggressively hacking away at hard, unyielding stone all day. The association of stone with the male world makes an obvious point that requires little amplification. Masculine brute strength is required for the work in the quarry. Any touch of feminine softness or feeling would be entirely out of place. Can you imagine a man complaining of fatigue here? Absolutely not, for such an admission would be seen as a sign of weakness—something that men are not encouraged by our culture to display. Whether we like to admit it or not, whether we are truly conscious of it or not, society is always in preparation for war and men, therefore, must be strong and tough—like stone.

It is in the Stonewall Quarry that the reader hears the first hint of masculine attitudes toward women. Cuyler's colleagues joke lewdly about his newlywed wife's physical amplitude (Mercy is a compulsive eater):

> As for his wife, well (this they said with a wink, a poke of the elbow), there's enough woman there to keep two or three fellows busy all night long. (24)

To these men, Mercy is an object (sexual at that) much like the stone, which they hack away at all day long. She is certainly not seen as a woman who provides thoughtful domestic comfort, nor is she respected as an interesting human being.

Cuyler Goodwill, a virgin when he marries, is portrayed as a man with "immense, unfathomable ardor" for his bride (7). Passionately he declares to Mercy, "I love you. Oh, how I love you with all my heart" (16). Such ardor is heartening to the reader but, on careful scrutiny of Cuyler's behavior, one recognizes more of a heated lust of the loins than a tender love of the heart. As Theodore Reik says in *Of Love and Lust,* "Love is one of the most overworked words in our vocabulary" (9).

Love, a matter of the heart, is quite distinct from sex, an issue of the instincts, although it does not preclude it. Ideally, the sex act can be a good way of expressing tender feelings for another. But, our entire history of war has not encouraged men to make this kind of connection. As stated before, tenderness, empathy, and compassion have no place in warrior conditioning, which aims at turning men, effectively, into stone. Reik distinguishes sex from love: "Sex is a passionate interest in another body; love a passionate interest in another personality, or in his life" (21).

Cuyler Goodwill is passionately interested in his wife's body. Returning home from the stone quarry every evening, he anticipates her delicious physical availability. During the day, as he chips away at the stone, his thoughts revolve around Mercy. But does he reminisce about certain adored qualities of her personality—her sweet smile perhaps, or her delightful childlike innocence? No indeed. Instead, "the tidal motion of sexual longing fills him to the brim" (35); he thinks of "his Mercy, the creases and secrets of her body, her fleshy globes and clefts, her hair, her scent, her way of turning toward him, offering herself" (34). We never hear about the couple simply holding hands, or exchanging thoughts and experiences during moonlight walks. There is no evidence in the novel of true intimacy—a revelation of soul to soul. Nor is there any sign that Cuyler is concerned for, let alone aware of, his wife's true feelings. He realizes that her ardor is "of a quality inferior to his own" (33), but this does not stop his regular nightly forays into her ample body. Mercy bears some responsibility for Cuyler's ignorance because she plays the man's game, pretending (or attempting to pretend) some degree of pleasure, as women have been taught to do. In reality, she is mildly bewildered and embarrassed by the entire sexual business. She also feels overwhelmed by the aggression of the act:

> Niagara in all its force is what she's reminded of as he climbs on top of her each evening, a thundering let loose against the folded interior walls of her body. (7)

Some might argue that Cuyler truly loves his wife. After all, he thinks of her and her alone—a fact that shows a strong attachment; and he is certainly not stingy with words of endearment. He also enjoys the comforts of home that Mercy provides for him—the meals, her big body warming his bed. But the focus and momentum of the relationship for Cuyler are strictly physical and center on his needs. Moreover, it is the sexual act alone that seems to loosen Cuyler's tongue:

> There in the sheeted width of their feather bed, his roughened male skin discovering the abundant soft flesh of his wife's body, enclosing it, entering it—that was the moment when the stone in his throat became dislodged. An explosion of self-forgetfulness set his tongue free. (85)

Self-forgetfulness, which is so central to genuine love, is limited here to the momentary explosion of sexual climax.

Unhappily for the Goodwills' neighbor, Clarentine Flett, sex does not go so far as to dislodge the stone in her husband's throat: Magnus Flett is "not a man who wasted words" (14). Overhearing Cuyler declare his passion for Mercy as she passes by the Goodwill home, Clarentine is astonished. She has read about "love talk, sweetheart talk" (17) in cheap novels, but her own experience has led her to believe that such words of endearment could not issue from ordinary quarry workers. Clarentine's husband is described as "a master stonecutter, a cold lean Orkneyman" whose "Orkney ways have stayed with him" (9). This means that he "prefers simple things":

> A plainly furnished house. A carefully tended garden. Ordinary food on the table, a supper of porridge or smoked fish or even a plate of bread and butter washed down by tea. (9)

In other words, Magnus is not the last of the big-time spenders. In fact, he is quite mean-spirited with his wife, who is described as a woman "half-crazed with menopause and loneliness and in mourning for her unlived life" (27). Asking her husband for the two dollars and fifty cents required to consult the local doctor about her painfully abscessed tooth, Clarentine is turned down with "soothing words" of hope that the infection will probably die down on its own. Obviously, Magnus is not concerned about his wife's pain or her health. Actually, machines are more important to him than his wife for he spends eleven dollars and shipping expenses for a new icebox—something that Clarentine has no need of and has never asked for. As he runs his fingers over the "New Improved Labrador Ice Chest" (15), an unwelcome thought occurs to Clarentine: "Those same fingers have touched me, my naked body" (15).

It is clear that Magnus's hands have not touched his wife gently since she assumes that "her husband was no rougher in his ways than other men." In fact, "his ways" can best be described as cold, perfunctory and mechanical—in short, stony:

> "If you're willing, Mother," he says in the darkness of their back bedroom, one hand working up her nightdress. A thousand times, five thousand times—"If you're willing,

> Mother." The words have worn a groove in her consciousness, she hardly hears them. And afterwards there's silence, like falling down a hole, or a kind of grunt that she takes to be satisfaction. (14)

Slam, bam—thank you, ma'am?

Lest anyone thinks that Magnus's unfeeling approach is limited to quarry workers, it should be stressed that Mercy's daughter Daisy receives similar treatment from her husband, Barker Flett, a senior civil servant. Awaiting the return of her husband from a business trip, Daisy anticipates his customary behavior:

> Her husband will be home in an hour or so, having in his usual way taken a taxi from the station. He will remove his trousers in the dark bedroom, hanging them neatly over the back of the chair. . . . Then his tie, next his shirt and underwear. Then, unaware of her tears wetting the blanket binding and the depth of her loneliness, he will lie down on top of her, being careful not to put too much weight on her frame ("A gentleman always supports himself on his elbows"). His eyes will be shut, and his warm penis will be produced and directed inside her, and then there

> will be a few minutes of rhythmic rocking. (191)

Like her mother before her and countless other women, Daisy will acquiesce but not without realizing, at some level, that something is seriously amiss with a culture that expects the woman to respond with ardor to such perfunctory, unemotional coupling:

> On and on it will go while Mrs. Flett [Daisy] tries, as through a helix of mixed print and distraction, to remember exactly what was advised in the latest issue of *McCalls,* something about a wife's responsibility for demonstrating a rise in ardor; that was it—ardor and surrender expressed simultaneously through a single subtle gesturing of the body; but how was that possible? (191)

One can only agree with the conclusion (whether it is the author's or Daisy's): "That men and women should be bound to each other in this way! How badly reality is organized" (192).

The absence of true intimacy between men and women in *The Stone Diaries* brings to mind two paintings, recently exhibited at a local library, which visually captured this sad state of affairs. In the picture to the left, a man and woman sit back to back on a plank-like bench; the woman's head and part of her upper body are turned around, reaching toward her partner; his body remains stiff and aloof, leaning forward and away from her, elbow raised in a defensive position. Immediately to the right of this painting hung another by the same artist: a voluptuous mother nurses her infant, while her young son of about eight years scampers away from her with a phallic flute to his lips. Running from the intimate scene behind him, the boy turns his back on his first true love and begins his flight into masculinity. Unconscious warrior conditioning of the male begins early and continues to obstruct intimacy throughout his lifetime.

As we have seen in *The Stone Diaries*, a novel that reflects reality, the heart is missing in human sexual connection. Without a genuine feeling of love for the woman, without a heartfelt, caring appreciation of her value as a human personality, the act is as mechanistic and as ugly as a modern musical composition sans melody. We are simply left with the impression of a rutting animal. Is it so strange then that Caroline Flett, as she watches her husband stroke the new icebox, does not welcome the thought that those same fingers have touched her naked body?

Speaking of mechanical treatment brings to mind a recent concert during which a modern composition was wedged into an otherwise beautiful program consisting of two exquisitely moving works by Felix Mendelssohn and a Haydn Trumpet Concerto. The contemporary piece seemed to be stuck into the program, as if by design, to illustrate the imbalance and ugliness of our time. Thank God, the raucous, dissonant modern work was almost as brief as the sexual forays portrayed in *The Stone Diaries.* The composer, a very attractive young woman, was acclaimed on stage with flowers and applause, thus demonstrating "lip service" appreciation of the feminine in a predominantly male field. But there was no sign of the feminine in the music for, like most modern music, it lacked melody, which is the element that stirs our deeper feelings. Without melody there is no beauty in music; in fact, music ceases to be music in the usual sense. The proverbial phrase, "music soothes the savage breast," refers to the healing, inspiring and nurturing impact of music on our souls. Today's classical music does not soothe, nor does it exalt; it reflects, rather, the complete invasion of the culture by masculine mechanistic values. Melody has vanished and with it, feeling and beauty. We are left with a collection of harsh, grinding sounds, not unlike those of a noisy factory—slam, bam, thank you, ma'am. Sitting in the concert hall, I felt politely violated and was tempted to make a quick exit. Interestingly, but not surprisingly, most of the audience seemed to listen politely and applauded at the end. It would appear that we are prepared to dupe ourselves about modern music in much the same way as we refuse to face up to the absence of beauty and genuine emotional intimacy in sexual relationships.

Although there is a general blindness to the absence of true intimacy, there is an awareness that something is seriously amiss in the relationships between men and women. While the desire to mate for life persists, the current staggering levels of divorce can hardly be overlooked. In fact, a recent issue of *Time* featured a study of this contemporary phenomenon which refuses to improve.

It is also difficult to ignore the proliferation of material offering "how to" solutions. Cast your eye around—at newsstands, movies, television—and you are sure to find people struggling with issues of sexuality. Unfortunately, in its focus on sex as the central locus of relationships, our culture is barking up the wrong tree. Tuning into television, a medium of great value as an accurate indicator of cultural problems and values, one can frequently see young couples who air their marital problems on talk shows. Repeatedly, wives complain here that they do not enjoy sex because they are usually too tired and their husbands climb on and off their bodies, regardless. What kind of solutions are offered? Well, there is the example of a forty-fivish blond woman who draws the unhappy couples' attention to a book she has just written on how to have better sex. Like a Greek chorus, she chants "sex is the glue that keeps a marriage together" and "women need to have orgasms." Just what dispirited couples need to hear. People are sure to get stuck with that kind of glue. Indeed, they are not likely to get close to any kind of *real* human relationship with such a narrow approach.

Like a needle stuck in an old-fashioned phonograph record, the refrain sounds over and over again that the answer to better relationships lies in better sex for both partners, which in turn is supposed to depend on better technique. Patrick Carnes, in his study *Don't Call It Love: Recovery From Sexual Addiction,* calls attention to the fact that our entire culture is so confused about sexuality that it supports a widespread addiction to sex. "Commercials, television, movies—all media support it," says Dr. Carnes. We have all seen nearly-naked couples, intertwined and devouring each other, on television and movie screens. Frequently interrupted by seductive young women advertising anything from condoms to cosmetics, these images suggest that sex is the source of happiness and well-being. Is it any wonder that the vast majority of the population looks to improved sex as the solution to unhappy marital relationships? As a result of this kind of misguided sexual idolatry, "how to" manuals abound, couples seek sex counseling, and often watch other panting couples in pornographic films, in order to learn technique and to experience a "turn-on." Men suffering from impotence turn to penile implants and Viagra as panaceas. Weight control mogul Susan Powter's famous refrain, "Stop the insanity," seems fitting here.

Our culture's obsession with sex and sexual mechanics is terribly misguided because it is exclusively masculine in orientation and overlooks the essential emotional element in human relationships. There are two major areas in life, the world of invention and of human relations. Mistakenly, because of the overevaluation of the masculine principle, we look to men for standards and guidance in both areas. Even women buy into masculine outlooks. The fact that men are accomplished in the world of ideas and machines, however, does not indicate an expertise in relationships and love. If this were so, obviously war as a method of resolving difficulties would not exist.

The antagonistic mode of war, however, does persist and has done so from the beginning of recorded time. It is the ongoing threat of war that thwarts the emotional development of men. As we have said before, the constant spectre of war goes hand in hand with the warrior conditioning of males. One cannot kill another human being if connecting feelings of empathy and compassion exist. The cost of war in terms of human lives is obvious; the cost in human relationship between men and women is equally serious. Men are left with sex as a substitute for emotional intimacy, and this counterfeit intimacy is foisted, unthinkingly, on society simply because it is the highly valued masculine way.

The truth is that sex is merely an instinct; it is not good or bad. At its best, however, it can be a beautiful instrument for the expression of love. But, as an instinct, it needs to be left alone. The more an instinct is focused on, worried about and taken out of all context, the more perverse it becomes. Men and women are not merely animals. If they can relate to each other in an empathetic, caring way, the sexual aspect will fall into place naturally and effortlessly. Sex is certainly not the glue in a marriage, but *caring* love is. Love, however, involves the baring of souls, the expression of genuine feelings, the acknowledgment of one's human vulnerability. It involves the willingness to serve another human being in much the same way as a mother protectively serves her child. At the same time, it involves the ability to disclose one's inner child seeking nurturance. After all, we never completely grow out of the early stage. As things stand, our culture does not encourage men to show their feelings of vulnerability. Instead, as I have said before, they must remain tough and strong.

Although sex in itself is not the glue in a marriage, the act of sexual intercourse does epitomize the quality of a relationship or the lack of it. In her attempt to underscore the insensitive treatment of women by men in an act that should serve an intimate relationship, Andrea Dworkin examines Tolstoy's novella, *The Kreutzer Sonata,* as a paradigm of sexual reality. The book is largely autobiographical and, as Dworkin points out, "crazed with misogyny and insight" (4). Central to the story is its analysis of the nature of sexual intercourse and marriage. Considered by many to be one of Tolstoy's strangest works, and censored by the state over one hundred years ago, *The Kreutzer Sonata* is particularly interesting because it offers an articulate and candid masculine point of view. We have already mentioned Sophie Tolstoy's distress in her marriage to an apparently pitiless and insensitive husband. In *The Kreutzer Sonata,* we get to know the thinly-disguised, guilt-ridden man himself.

The story recounts the confession of Pozdnuishef, a well-to-do gentleman who has murdered his wife in a fit of jealousy.

Acquitted by a court, which accepts this crime as a justifiable defense of male honor, the protagonist tries to explain his act to himself and to a fellow passenger on a train. Pozdnuishef locates the root of his tragic act in the social conditioning of men to use women as sexual objects of pleasure. Conveyed exclusively to men in Tolstoy's time, the notion that sex was a health necessity gave them licence to prioritize the carnal nature of the act rather than its moral and spiritual dimensions. Sexual satisfaction for the male clearly took precedence over any issue of relationship and commitment. Women, on the other hand, were expected to retain their virginity until marriage. It is interesting to note that with the sexual revolution in the nineteen sixties, the double standard vanished and the foolish notion of sex as a health necessity was extended to women as well. Women accepted this "privilege" as a wonderful freedom formerly denied to them.

Pozdnuishef, in retrospect, realizes that a purely sensual approach to the opposite sex is depraved and, to use a word that he repeats throughout the novel, "swinish." In her discussion of *The Kreutzer Sonata,* Dworkin recapitulates Pozdnuishef's argument in which he recognizes the general impairment of the male's ability to love:

> The loss of innocence—the loss of virginity for a man already socialized to exploit—is a real and irreversible corruption of his capacity to love a human being as an individual. The depravity of being a calloused exploiter is what he brings to the marriage bed as a whole. (12)

Pozdnuishef 's depravity is, indeed, largely responsible for a tortured relationship with his wife from courtship until her death. Although sexual intercourse is compulsive, frequent and intense, the marriage is loveless. Pozdnuishef foists himself on his wife regardless of her feelings, her frequent pregnancies, and her fatigue caused by nursing her infants. Moreover, he feels, arrogantly, that he has a right to exploit his wife's body as his personal possession. In the period between sexual encounters, Pozdnuishef feels anger, revulsion and resentment toward his wife, rather than tender love. From the very beginning of their marriage, the couple finds easy communication impossible; genuine intimacy is completely absent. Neither husband nor wife is content in the marriage, but the union endures.

A dramatic change occurs when Madame Pozdnuishef, for the sake of her health, is advised against further pregnancies. Learning birth control methods, the woman is freed from the risky burden of further child-bearing. Like a flower suddenly transported to healthier soil, she flourishes, growing more beautiful than ever. Flowers, however, require ample light and water as well as good soil. Seeking the loving, considerate attention denied to her by her husband, the lady's gaze wanders and lights on an ardent musician who courts her. Pozdnuishef informs the reader that behind every sentimental lover lies, in reality, a predatory, sensual male but, obviously, his wife is not privy to this insight.

Highly suspicious of his wife, the husband returns prematurely from a business trip to find her with the musician, dining in her quarters. Dagger in hand, Pozdnuishef attacks, the lover flees, and the wife is stabbed to death. It is significant that the husband momentarily sees his wife as human only after he has brutally murdered her:

> I looked at the children and at her bruised and disfigured face, and for the first time I forgot myself, my

> rights, my pride and for the first time saw a human being in her. (117)

Andrea Dworkin points to the "heart of the contradiction, the internal tension at the center of this sexual system of value and cognition:"

> . . . alive, in rebellion, flesh he is near and inside of, she is not human; with her dead, more object-like than human, his pain is ended and he recognizes her, for one moment, as human—perhaps because she is now someone he no longer needs to fuck. (18)

Another way of seeing Pozdnuishef 's reaction might take into consideration the fact that with intimacy no longer a threat in terms of exposed vulnerability, he can afford to recognize his wife as a human being.

With hindsight, Pozdnuishef realizes that the murder of his wife did not consist of a single act of violent rage:

> They thought I killed her with a dagger on the seventeenth of October. I did not kill her then; it was long before. In exactly the same way that men are killing their wives right now, all, all. (45-46)

Tolstoy's fictional husband proceeds to explain that he killed his wife slowly, throughout the marriage, by his arrogant and inconsiderate sexual exploitation of her body. To the sensitive reader, it is obvious that Pozdnuishef's lust for his wife lacked empathy and compassion. There could be no genuine intimacy. Truly, Tolstoy portrays sexual intercourse as an abusive act committed by men.

As stated previously, Pozdnuishef traces the root of his abusive behavior to a social conditioning, which cripples the male's humanity via the encouragement of sexual exploitation of woman. He sees, further, that this attitude dictates the assumption that women are inferior to men despite any legal and social gains:

> So it is with the emancipation of women. The slavery of woman consists in precisely this, that men choose to take advantage of her as an instrument of enjoyment and consider it right to do so. Well, and now they emancipate woman, they give her all the same rights as men, but they still regard her as an instrument of enjoyment, so they educate her, both in childhood and later by public opinion, with this end in view. But she remains the same depraved slave as before and her husband the same depraved slave-owner.

> They emancipate woman in the colleges and in the law courts, but they still look on her as an object of enjoyment. Train her, as she is trained among us, to regard herself in this light, and she will always remain a lower creature. (50-51)

Tolstoy's genius and honesty, as it reveals itself in his character's insight, is well worth listening to in our own liberated era. Unfortunately, men still view women as sexual objects, thanks to their warrior conditioning, which inhibits full emotional involvement. Speaking in this vein, Pozdnuishef seems sympathetic toward the plight of woman.

Tolstoy's protagonist, however, often exhibits a misogyny which appears to stem from a somewhat paranoid conviction that women take revenge on men by making themselves as attractive and seductive as possible. From his masculine point of view, the exploited enslave the exploiters by playing the man's game. Denied fully human status, woman acquires the power to dominate man simply because he has great need of her sexual services. Trust a man to think of everything from the standpoint of power. It is precisely the perceived power of his wife that enrages

Pozdnuishef throughout his marriage. Clearly, he cannot tolerate his dependence on her. Finally, faced with the possibility of his wife's adultery, he cannot avoid the fact that her body does not belong to him, that he cannot control it:

> It was horrible: I claimed an absolute right to her body just as if it had been my own body; at the same time I was aware that I could not control that body of hers, that it was not mine, that she had the power to dispose of it as she wished. (102)

The recognition of his complete helplessness in the face of his wife's desire to seek love elsewhere causes Pozdnuishef an unbearable anguish that ends only with his killing her.

Predicated as it is solely on the power principle, which is impelled by an inability to tolerate helpless feelings, Pozdnuishef's tale presents the masculine point of view *par excellence*. It is the story of countless husbands, who like Tolstoy, Mahler and the fictitious husbands in Carol Shield's Pulitzer Prize winning novel, thoughtlessly and with no *mal entente,* use their wives as objects of release and questionable pleasure. As Karl Stern states in *The Flight From Woman,* "The regard for the human person in terms of use and disposal is the male fallacy" (286). *Logos,* the rational male principle, when not balanced by the empathic and compassionate feelings of the feminine *Eros,* results in a heartless approach to other human beings. Assertion of power is the rule here.

In his book, *The Male Ego,* Willard Gaylin mentions the obvious link between warrior conditioning of men and their impetus to power: "Man must be a warrior. He must be powerful and he must demonstrate his powers whether he lives in a hunting or a non-hunting society" (41). Gaylin quotes the "somewhat paranoid" (76) views of French sociologist Emmanuel Reynaud on the general male approach to relationships:

> Relations between men center around the struggle for power; whether individually or in a group, they are permanent rivals in the appropriation of women, wealth, and glory. Friendship, so often proclaimed as a typically masculine sentiment is more of a pact of non-aggression, a brief respite from the fight. (76)

Somewhat paranoid or not, Reynaud's assessment certainly acknowledges the antagonistic, non-intimate warrior stance of masculine behavior. His description of the male sexual foray repeats the power theme:

> Man does not generally envisage relationships other than as power relations. He chases, approaches or seduces a woman to conquer her; the language he uses is revealing and sounds more like that of a sailor, hunter or warrior than of a lover. A woman is not a person to be discovered, but a body to be undressed. (77)

It is interesting that Reynaud's perspective parallels that of Tolstoy's killer husband in *The Kreutzer Sonata.* For the sake of a balanced view, however, it should be said that not all men are tarred with the same brush. Thankfully, some do have a tender caring side, in spite of social conditioning.

Gaylin draws attention to the crucial importance of the early separation of the young male from his mother and any identification with her female qualities in preparation for "real" manhood:

> Men must avoid all the threatening implications of female-like behavior. The essential goal in becoming a real man is to liberate one's self from the previous feminine identification with

> the mother. To be a real man we must stop being a "mama's boy," since a crucial stage in male development . . . demands abandoning the primary identification with the mother. (30)

Clearly, the denial of feminine qualities for the sake of tough warrior manhood ("to be a real man") is costly in terms of a more humane manhood. The two paintings mentioned earlier come to mind again: The contemporary and highly mechanistic portrait of a man and woman, seated back to back on a bench, and immediately next to it, the picture of a young boy, flute in hand, running away from his nursing mother. Although the artist may not have had this in mind consciously, it is as if the second painting, in which the boy turns his back on his first, and perhaps only, genuine intimate relationship, explains the lack of closeness in the first.

As long as the underlying fabric of society is woven with the pattern of war, men will not be encouraged to develop toward wholeness by giving full play to their feminine emotional side. As Emma Jung points out in *Animus and Anima,* "Up to now in our world, the feminine principle, as compared to the masculine, has always stood for something inferior" (23).

To accept any kind of softer feeling behavior on the part of men involves the acceptance of "what is regarded as less valuable, what is weak, passive, subjective, illogical, bound to nature—in a word, femininity" (41). Men would have to descend from a position of pride to accept these qualities as part of their psychological makeup—a difficult undertaking, to say the very least. It is a far easier and more exciting task for women to achieve balance by developing the highly regarded masculine characteristics as, in fact, they have been doing.

Balance is required for humanity to move forward creatively. Dominated exclusively by the masculine principle, as we are, we race toward Armageddon. Had we been dominated in the past by the feminine, we would never have advanced, in all likelihood, to the marvelous degree of technological comfort and ease that our contemporary world provides. To quote Emma Jung again:

> There are many women who have developed their powers of thinking, discrimination and criticism to a high degree, but there are very few who are mentally creative in the way a man is. It is maliciously said that woman is

> so lacking in the gift of invention that if the kitchen spoon had not been invented by a man, we would today still be stirring the soup with a stick! (21)

Madame Jung was hardly a mental slouch herself. She does not denigrate women but, rather, sees that their creativity finds expression "in the sphere of living," "in the shaping of life generally" and in "the development of relationships" (21) which are so essential to life.

It bears emphasizing that a balance of masculine and feminine modes, individually and globally, is the way to ensure the survival of the species. Where the masculine dominates, there is the will to power. As Karl Stern reminds us, "All true love for another means a renunciation—painful or effortless, conscious or unconscious, intentional or unintentional—of power. (Inversely, all power over another is an impairment of love)" (277).

Nowadays we can see as never before that the peril which threatens all of us comes not from nature, but from man, from the psyches of the individual and the mass. The psychic aberration of man is the danger. Everything depends upon whether or not our psyche functions properly. If certain persons lose their heads nowadays, a hydrogen bomb will go off.

There is the general feeling, to be sure, that we have reached a significant turning point in the ages, but people imagine that the great change has to do with nuclear fission and fusion, or with space rockets. What is concurrently taking place in the human psyche is usually overlooked.

C.G. Jung,
Memories, Dreams, Reflections

Of the Apollonian-Dionysian conflict in antiquity, Koepgen says it found its solution in Christianity because "in the person of Jesus the male is united with the female."

Carl Jung quoting
from Georg Koepgen,
Die Gnosis des Christentums, 1939

Chapter Six

Androgyny or Perish!

In a remarkable essay about the Catholic dogma of the Assumption of Mary, Graham Greene points out that Mary, the Mother of God, is the only perfect image of human love. As Greene notes, Mary alone of all the saints in the Church is never associated with punishment. The concept of justice is equally foreign to her, yielding instead to compassion and love (81). As the symbolic essence of caring, understanding and nurturance, Mary represents the ideal feminine principle which is maternal.

The sheer weight of architectural and artistic glory that has been inspired in the past by the simplest of women is awesome. It is interesting that the image of Mary continues to appear in our age, which has less time for her than former eras. Not only do visions of Mary appear to simple folk and children, but she continues to inspire artists. Recently, an article headed, "Memory of Virgin Mary Mobilizes Creation," appeared in a widely-read newspaper.* The article describes a contemporary chapel, designed by Italian artist Anzo Cuachi and Swiss architect Mario Botta, destined for dedication to *Santa Maria degli Angeli.* Feminine in form, the welcoming shrine, which hugs the earth, is described as "a circular edifice." Bare but not stiff, it is to be "a space of hard spiritual calm, yet one that certainly will be restful to any soul inundated by the mass-cultural deluge of commodities and images." Clearly, we need, today more than ever, the comforting, restorative embrace of the maternal in our speedy, stressful, unbalanced lives.

The feminine relational approach to life, though visible down through recorded history, has never been esteemed enough to balance the masculine. Power, equated with the masculine impulse, has always taken precedence over caring love and compassion as the ruling principle of

* Globe and Mail, Saturday, 23 September 1995, C5.

the world. With the present scientific-technological burst of human creativeness, the feminine has been all but eclipsed. Mankind's power over matter has currently extended into the sphere of human relationships with the result that people are viewed as expendable objects.

Lacking our intuitive connection with the natural world we become detached robots, no longer part of nature but isolated machines. As inventors of inanimate devices, which indeed serve us greatly, we become part of our work. This is, after all, the inevitable outcome of a very involved kind of enterprise. Yes, as inventors we become like the machines we bring into existence—cold, separated from the natural world about us, and incapable of perceiving its beauty. In short, a state of frigidity results that is totally alien to genuine, wholesome lives as human beings. Since we raise our children in such a society, it is small wonder that many become destructive, cold-blooded creatures, lacking pity or remorse, bent on filling the empty emotional tank they sense in themselves with whatever fuel they may find. Often enough, alienation results in a kind of destructive excitement, intent on escape from a cold, detached environment.

There is a well-known phrase from the greatest psychologist of all time, William Shakespeare: "All the world's a stage,/ And all the men and women merely players." Could this statement not be brought up to date and rephrased as, "All the world's a machine and the men and women merely mechanics?" This abysmal state of affairs is the end result of the loss of the feminine half of life, leading universally to a serious loss of balance—a kind of mass psychosis. Without the maternal influence to balance the masculine, the sacredness of individual life vanishes from view and human beings become mere ciphers in a cold, objectified, homeless world.

The wanton mass destruction of innocent people in Hiroshima and Nagasaki at the end of World War II offers vivid evidence of the callous masculine approach to human life. Most historians say that at the highest levels of the Truman administration, morality never entered the discussion over the decision to use atomic warfare twice in a row. By August 6th, 1945, dozens of Japanese and German cities had been leveled by conventional bombing in an attempt to shock the enemy into surrender. Apparently, the atomic weapons dropped on Hiroshima and Nagasaki just looked like a more efficient manner of accomplishing the same result.

I used to wonder if the men in charge of this murderous enterprise could have executed their mission if they had pictured the men, women and children of the two Japanese cities going innocently about their morning activities. Could they have dropped the atomic bombs if they had envisioned the ghastly inferno they were to unleash? Sadly, an answer came one evening as I watched a member of the Enola Gay (the airplane carrier of the first atomic bomb used in World War II) being interviewed on television. He admitted that he subsequently saw the ravages of the bomb—the complete devastation of the city, twisted steel and mangled bodies and body parts, as well as photos of survivors with skin and flesh peeling from their bodies. Yes, he was troubled by the deaths of so many children. He liked kids, and had grandchildren of his own by the time of the interview. From his point of view, it was all very tragic. When asked specifically, "Have you felt any remorse about your involvement in that holocaust?" he replied firmly, "No, none whatsoever!" Moreover, this elderly military official reported that no one involved in the decision to drop the bomb felt an ounce of guilt or regret. It was simply something that had to be done to end the war quickly and emphatically. I was reminded of a number of Nazi officers in charge of the systematic slaughter of millions of human beings in concentration camps who are remembered by their grandchildren as kindly, responsible family men.

In 1952, Hollywood gave Americans what it called "The story of a brave man and the woman who loved him." The movie delivered a clear moral message: War is hell, but not doing your duty is worse. *Above and Beyond* was a film about Paul Nibbits, the pilot of the Enola Gay. (Ironically, the airplane that delivered the first atomic bomb was named after Nibbits mother!) In a touching scene, Nibbits and his wife gaze at their sleeping children. The sight of her little ones tucked safely into their beds fills Lucy Nibbits with a profound sadness. She agrees with her husband that their children are wonderful but, at the same time, expresses concern and compassion for all the children facing death in war-torn, enemy countries: "Oh, I keep thinking about this war and how somewhere, at this very moment, bombs are being dropped and children like ours are being killed." Her husband commands sharply, "Lucy, don't ever say that again—not to me! " and proceeds to "clear up a little piece of morality." "It's not bombs alone that are harmful," he lectures. "It's war—war is what's wrong, not just weapons. Sure we're in a war, innocent people are dying and it's horrible. But to lose this war to the gang we're fighting would be the most immoral thing we could do to those kids in there. And don't you ever forget it!" Clearly, winning at all costs takes precedence over the sanctity of human life.

Obviously, the only antidote to war and its callous disregard for the sacredness of each and every individual is the feminine maternal attitude of empathy and compassion that Lucy Nibbits exemplifies. As I have mentioned before, Karl Stern states that "The regard for the human person in terms of use and disposal is the male fallacy, as it were" (286). He offers the example of Dostoevsky's protagonist, Raskolnikov, from the novel *Crime and Punishment*. An unsuccessful law student mired in poverty, Raskolnikov is obsessed with power. Consequently, he plans the murder of an old, mercenary pawnbroker in order to convince himself that he has a touch of greatness, which puts him beyond the moral limits of ordinary mortals. As he confesses to his girlfriend Sonya, the murder is an experimental case. Raskolnikov purposely chooses a victim whose life is, ostensibly, "of no use." When he tells Sonya "I've only killed a louse Sonya, a useless, loathsome, harmful creature." Her horrified reaction, "A human being—a louse!" could have been the response, as Stern notes, "of millions of mothers in countless wars and purges" (287).

The movie *Above and Beyond* and Dostoevsky's novel are just two works of art among many that illustrate the contrast between the feminine heart and the masculine lack of it. Chaim Potok's moving novel, *I Am the Clay,* offers a more contemporary example of this dichotomy. In the midst of the horror of the Korean War, an old man and his wife, fleeing from invading Chinese and North Korean soldiers, embark upon a nomadic trek along the main road to Seoul. Scrambling into a roadside ditch to avoid an approaching column of American tanks and jeeps, they find a severely wounded young boy whose parents have just been killed. The old woman refuses to leave the boy behind in their flight through the bleak bombed-out landscape, and with a fierce maternal devotion she nurses the child back to health. In contrast, the old man thinks his wife is out of her mind to put their lives at risk for a stranger. He sees the orphan as a stone around their necks and a threat to his own meager food supply. Silently, torn by rage and jealousy, he hopes for the boy's death.

Stern reminds us that the disregard for human life is inimical to the feminine involvement with bringing life into this world:

> Wherever individuals become ciphers, the feminine is wounded. For on the purely natural level—apart from the question of Grace, or even apart from all theological or philosophic reflection—the sense of the infinite importance of the single individual is rooted in the experience of pregnancy, birth and nursing. Scripture and theology teach us that the world was created for Man to dwell in. But while someone is reading this line, a woman gives birth, with that immediate sense of certainty that the world has been created for this particular new human being. This certainty is not the result

> of abstraction. It arises out of an irreducible fusion with creative being. Hence the calculus of human logistics, that horrid concept of the human "material," which can be thought of as usable and as expendable, is forever inimical to the feminine. (286)

Certainly, any woman who has given birth to an infant after carrying it in her womb for nine months will assent to Stern's appreciation of the woman's reverence for life. But the experience itself is not required for a nurturing attitude to life. The woman's entire biology, under normal circumstances, provides the focus of relatedness.

The birth process, however, is a profound and excruciating experience in which mother and infant share the most desolate feelings of pain and helplessness. Some years ago, the distinguished Viennese psychoanalyst Marta Wassermann, when interviewed on the radio by an upbeat, sunny woman who chirped "I was born with a happy heart," replied realistically, if not caustically, "We are all born crying out in our unspeakable discomfort." As a matter of fact, the trauma of birth is a topic extensively covered in psychiatry, particularly by psychoanalysts.

The concept is described comprehensively by Otto Rank, who maintained that the experience of birth is deeply imprinted upon the psyche of the infant and often shows up in symbolic form in the associations of patients. The act of being born marks a radical upheaval indeed from both psychic and physical points of view; it produces a great shock, a trauma from which the person is never reconciled. It is easy to understand that the expulsion by nature from the warm, enveloping comfort of amniotic fluid in the womb into the cold, harsh, unsupportive reality of a separate existence is an utterly miserable experience for every human being. We are born completely helpless, unable to do anything for ourselves, and the only saving grace is the comforting response of the mother—her empathetic countenance, voice, embrace, and response to our needs! Our very survival, emotional and physical, depends on her caring intuitive response.

The mother can relate to the infant's vulnerability all the more easily because she herself has suffered helplessly. We do not fully realize today that giving birth is a matter of life and death. Before the advent of modern medicine, countless women died in the process and infants orphaned at birth were commonplace. Although the situation has greatly improved, the woman is still as helpless as the infant when, during delivery, nature takes over completely. She is swept along through painful contractions until she loses all sense of herself as a distinct ego in the final "bearing down" stage. The woman in labor is a mere vehicle of nature, a victim of fate. Her conditioning for this essentially powerless role begins in adolescence with the onset of menstruation. In fact, many women recalling their first menses have expressed a common response: terror at the possibility of hemorrhaging to death!

Helplessness is the fundamental condition, the rock-bottom root of all humankind. We are born in that state and we spend a large part of our lives dependent on the caring service of our mothers. We have no choice in these matters. If we live long enough, we face the erosion of our physical powers and ultimately the inevitability of death. Between birth and death, we know not what natural catastrophes await us. Perhaps no one articulates the essential helplessness of the human condition so eloquently as Freud in *The Future of an Illusion:*

> There are elements which seem to mock at all human control: the earth, which quakes, is rent asunder, and buries man and all his works; the water, which in tumult floods and submerges all things; the storm, which drives all before it; there are the diseases, which we have only lately recognized as the attacks of other living creatures; and finally there is the painful riddle of death, for which no remedy at all has yet been found, nor probably ever will be. With these forces nature rises up before us, sublime, pitiless inexorable; thus she brings again to mind our weakness and helplessness, of which we thought the work of civilization had rid us. (23)

Unlike women, men are not conditioned by nature to endure their rudimentary helplessness. Consequently, terrified of such feelings, they are free to repress them unconsciously, along with early memories of childhood vulnerability. This facility enables them, all the more easily, to pursue mastery over their environment with accompanying illusions of power. "To strive, to seek, to find, and not to yield," proclaims Tennyson's aging Ulysses, and readers all over the world thrill to such words of strength and grim determination.

Generally, men like to feel in charge of events and when control fails, they rage. Behind the rage is panic: they cannot tolerate the feeling of helplessness. Addressed to his dying father, Dylan Thomas's poem, *"Do Not Go Gently Into the Night,"* exemplifies a common masculine reaction to the inevitability of death, before which we are all helpless: "Rage, rage against the dying of the light," exhorts the poet repeatedly. Resignation of one's self to fate is not encouraged in this poem; throughout, Thomas extends the masculine heroic mode to its logical end—rage. What is war but rage, the masculine denial of helplessness?

There is no doubt that men, striving, seeking, and not yielding, have accomplished wonderful things. Faced with the problems of sheer physical survival, masculine determination and inventiveness have been necessary and valuable. Understandably, this aspect of life has assumed priority. The prevalence of the masculine, however, has brought us to an extreme crisis. Without the feeling side of human existence as a balance, we are mechanizing ourselves to death. The feminine caring mode, epitomized by empathy and compassion, is as important (if not more so) as the masculine, yet it has always been pushed aside, neglected and devalued. Feelings have been viewed as nice but not particularly significant. Trivialized, of course, they can be reduced to facile sentiment and romantic love.

The emotional side of life is easy to overlook in a world immersed in and obsessed with material advantages. Feelings are not tangible; we cannot touch them, see them as concrete objects, or buy them. Furthermore, they can be, at times, extremely painful because they remind us of our human vulnerability. After all, the feelings which join us to each other can be easily hurt when exposed. As much as we would all, in our common hubris, like to overlook the emotional realm from time to time, we cannot afford to continue this oversight. Frankly, life is not worth living without the world of feelings. We can have all the technology in the world, but without a warm, emotional pulse, life is a cold, dead reality. As I have said, without this crucial dimension we are all alienated ciphers, disembodied ghosts. Anyone who doubts this truth is advised to read the works of Franz Kafka, a writer who was able to portray this kind of cold alienation. Warning: these works of art are extremely depressing.

Make no mistake, we are rapidly moving to the point where there will be no human warmth and contact in the world. Lately, there have been predictions of a future replacement of service people by robots. We are not too far away from that dismal reality. Who has not had the experience of hearing a recorded voice on the telephone directing us to "Press 1 if you require . . ." or "Press 2 if you require service in English," etc. The latest advance in this direction came my way when I dialed a shopping club and heard "Hi, I'm Tina, your automated order processor." My own feeling of despair and disgust when greeted by a taped response rather than by a live, warm, helpful voice is surely a common one.

The present crisis, though incomparable in terms of potential universal catastrophe, is by no means unique. As Karl Stern notes, history professors have observed the parallels between our culture and that of the Roman Empire at its peak, prior to disintegration. Stern assesses the extreme imbalance that provided the setting for emerging Christianity:

> At the historical moment of the Incarnation, Roman civilization was under the sign of power, philosophy

> under the sign of unaided reason, and the visible church of the Old Covenant was in danger of formalism and ossification. (302)

In short, the masculine principle prevailed with no hint of compassion for the little people, the victims of those in power.

Significantly, this crisis in history opened the curtain to the drama of the Redemption and the appearance in Western mythology of Jesus Christ as the Messiah, along with the Blessed Virgin Mary.* From Carl Jung's perspective, myth is the revelation of a divine life in man, as well as a necessity because it gives meaning to life. Jung equates meaninglessness with illness:

> Meaninglessness inhibits fullness of life and is therefore equivalent to illness. Meaning makes a great many things endurable—perhaps everything. (*Memories* 340)

---

* From a Jungian perspective this great event was synchronistic. Jung describes synchronicity as a principle of non-causal connection. This means that there is some relationship between events that cannot be explained scientifically in terms of cause and effect. In fact, we have no way of explaining them, but they are meaningful coincidences nonetheless.

Jung understood that a myth, in order to be effective, must present "a view of the world which adequately explains the meaning of human existence in the cosmos" and that view must spring from "our psychic wholeness, from the co-operation between conscious and unconscious" (*Memories* 340).

The Christian myth, which Jung saw as one man's magnificent vision of the future, is certainly in the direction of wholeness since it elevates the feminine *eros* principle as a balance to and completion of the masculine *logos*. "Do not think that I have come to abolish the Law or the Prophets; I have not come to abolish them but to fulfill them," said Jesus (Matthew 5:17). He realized that without the element of compassion, the Hebrew Law was a hollow business leading to shallow hypocrisy.

Christ's message was (and still is) radical: He proclaimed and bore witness to a God of love. The God who prevailed throughout the Old Testament was a severe father, prone to anger, judgmental and punitive. Even if the earlier Bible did on occasion speak of the love of God, the image of God aroused fear more often than not. Indeed, not too many people who followed God's commandments felt His blessings shine upon them. Surely those exploited by the powerful leaders were unaware of the deity's favor. John the Baptist and his group inherited the severe Old Testament patriarchal image of God. His words contained the hint of God's judgment, His rage, His vengeance:

> O generation of vipers, who hath warned you to flee from the wrath to come? Bring forth therefore fruits meet for repentance. . . . And now also the axe is laid unto the root of the trees: therefore every tree which bringeth not forth good fruit is hewn down, and cast into the fire. (Matthew 3:7-10)

The message of Jesus proclaiming the gospel (good news) of God seems similar: "The time is fulfilled, and the kingdom of God is at hand: repent ye, and believe the gospel" (Mark 1:15). Both proclaim similar visions. John's, however, contains a terrifying threat of castigation while Jesus brings good news. Jesus makes no allusion to God's wrath and vengeance. Japanese author, Shusaku Endo, contrasts John's terrifying threats with the positive slant of the gospel of God announced by Jesus:

> Seeing these two proclamations side by side, we are captivated by the sense of how finally a new light is added to the most obscure vision of the Old Testament world. We get the impression of the long night being finished, the first streak of dawn breaking through. (45)

Endo provides an interpretation of Jesus somewhat at odds with the image possessed by American readers but close to my own. In his attempt to make Christianity more appealing to his own people, he tries "not so much to depict God in the father image that tends to characterize Christianity, but rather to depict the kindhearted maternal aspect of God revealed to us in the personality of Jesus" (1). The Jesus that Endo sees is "a person who lived for love and still more love," and who, nevertheless, was put to death "for he chose to live without violent resistance" (1).

I was reminded of this maternal aspect in the personality of Jesus recently during a performance of Handel's *Messiah*. Near the end of Part I, the alto and soprano sing what is for me the most exquisite music of the entire oratorio. Expressed with great feeling, the aria, which is gentle and tender, touches the heart. Handel's genius captures here the unique essence of Jesus which is, indeed, maternal. Borrowed from Matthew 11:28, the words together with the music convey the image of a caring, comforting, nurturing figure:

> He shall feed His flock like a shepherd and He shall gather the lambs with His arm, and carry them in His bosom and gently lead those that are with young. Come unto Him, all ye that labor and are heavy laden, and He will give you rest. Take His yoke upon you, and learn of Him, for He is meek and lowly of heart, and ye shall find rest unto your souls.

A recognition of the maternal aspect of Christ is consistent with Jung's approach to the figure of Jesus. Jung saw Christ as a symbol of the ideal Self. From his perspective, this highest development of mature individuation involved the concept of androgyny—a balance of gender opposites within the individual psyche. The concept of androgyny is often misunderstood as the absence of gender differences altogether, or else as a hermaphroditic state. *Au contraire,* Jung realized that the play of gender opposites visible in the world also takes place in the individual psyche, but with the obvious sexual identity we are born with at the helm of consciousness. The opposite gender exists as a potential balancing or compensating force in the person's unconscious. Thus, the unconscious of the male is the feminine *anima* and that of the female, the masculine *animus*. A highly evolved individual's psychological wholeness involves development and integration of the opposite side. Far from losing her/his obvious biological gender identity, such integration makes for a more rounded and balanced woman or man. Moreover, balance brings out the best of each side. William Phipps, a student of Christian history, points out that Jesus "surprised his companions by being both more 'feminine' and more 'masculine' than others" (80). This is not really surprising from a Jungian perspective since an androgynous balance is actually necessary for optimal performance of each pole.

In modern times, women generally have embraced their masculine side with enthusiasm. Indeed, the masculine principle is so overvalued that, at times, this side can take over to the detriment of the individual. As Emma Jung says in *Animus and Anima,* "Such a masculine training and way of life may well be achieved by identification with the animus, but then the feminine side is left out in the cold" (13). Madame Jung suggests an androgynous alternative:

> What is really necessary is that feminine intellectuality, logos in the woman, should be so fitted into the nature and life of the woman that a harmonious cooperation between the feminine and masculine factors ensues and no part is condemned to a shadowy existence. (13)

Men, generally, have been loath to develop their feminine side for the obvious reason that this mode has never been esteemed by the culture. This unfathomed psychological territory is, in fact, the man's soul (*anima* is the Italian word for soul). The male has seldom been comfortable with any acknowledgment of dependence and vulnerability, qualities traditionally associated with women. Understandably, he is far more at home with warrior positions of dominance and power. From a Jungian standpoint then, Jesus holds out universal hope for a more peaceful man of the future. William Phipps sees Jesus as the archetypal liberated man in the context of gender stereotypes (80).

As a man, Jesus possessed very pronounced masculine qualities. He was strong in body and had great stamina as a result of his trade as a carpenter or stonecutter. He courageously denounced the hypocrisy of the religious establishment and he drove the moneylenders from the Jerusalem temple. As an outstanding rabbi, he showed great intellect, keen wit, astute judgement and wisdom. But Jesus, obviously, was not caught up in the power principle for he was motivated by compassionate love and he dedicated his life to this maternal principle. There are so many instances in the Gospels of the compassion Jesus felt for the victims and outcasts of society. He loved children above all. He taught men the importance of assuming the servant's role, a role traditionally associated with women; and, like the good mother, he exemplified the virtue of self-sacrifice for others. The ability of Jesus to forgive rather than to harbor vengeful, castigating thoughts is perhaps the greatest illustration of his positive feminine side. Finding a group of men ready to stone an adulteress, he reminded them of their own feet of clay as he said, "He who is without sin among you, let him throw a stone at her first" (John 8:7). Jesus died on a final note of forgiveness which is truly unique. Suffering in agony on the cross, he nevertheless forgave his enemies ("Forgive them for they know not what they do.") because he realized that no one had really understood the crucial importance of his message.

Endo points out that the most striking feature in the passion narrative is the way that it, unhesitatingly, dares to spotlight "front and center stage" the helpless figure of Jesus. He sees the powerless, crucified Christ as a display of weakness:

> Jesus displayed on the cross nothing but utter helplessness and weakness. Nowhere does the passion narrative depict Jesus except in this utterly powerless image. (147)

Endo overlooks the real strength of Jesus on the cross. His strength does not fit the "manly" ideal associated with conquest which is, after all, superficial. It is the kind of strength that nature has endowed women with from the beginning—the strength to endure great suffering, to accept the fundamental helplessness of the human condition and the inevitability of destiny. No man could withstand the pain of childbirth as stoically and with so much love as women do. Jesus, in his ministry, knew what lay ahead. He accepted his destiny which he surely could have escaped. As the story tells us, He died for love, sacrificing his life for the salvation of humankind. In terms of *real* strength, the strength of resignation, Jesus was a giant.

It is doubtful that the men who saw Jesus die recognized his strength. Endo's reading of the gospels takes into account the popular disappointment engendered by the pacifist ways of this great figure. Jesus was viewed then as a weak, ineffectual, do-nothing disappointment by his peers. Suffering under Roman oppression, the Jews naturally looked for a strong militaristic messiah who would overthrow the Roman yoke. As Endo points out, men crave action, practical immediate results (119). Instead, Jesus spoke and lived the ways of love which include empathy, compassion, and forgiveness. According to the Gospels, no one really appreciated His message at the time.

The world has never moved very far from that position despite the emergence of Christendom in the Western World. As writers such as Walker Percy have emphasized, Christendom never practiced Christianity. In fact, the world has appreciated the truth exemplified by the symbol of

Jesus no more than it has valued the maternal role. Christ's message of love and compassion has not been absorbed by the male psyche. The chronic existence of war offers ample evidence of this reality. Caring love and compassion preclude killing.

While the androgynous ideal of Christ does offer direction and hope for the future, the cold, hard reality of Adolf Hitler serves as a warning of the danger inherent in the thrust of unbalanced masculinity. Obsessed with the idea of establishing a pure Aryan race and driven by the will to power, Hitler's heart was closed to the sacredness of human life. The man was seized by an idea that left no room for compassion. His unbridled masculinity is evident in his philosophy of war:

> The victor will not be asked later on, whether he told the truth or not. In starting and waging a war, it is not Right that matters but Victory. Have no pity. (Payne 355)

Victory at any cost! Certainly, Hitler and his henchmen had no pity for the millions of human beings, naked and stripped of all dignity, who were herded like cattle into gas chambers or shot to death in mass graves.

The epitome of evil, Hitler is regarded by many as the Antichrist. At one time, the German people saw him as their messiah. "When I met Hitler, I felt that I was face to face with God," said a German woman, recalling her first meeting with *der Fuerher.* In some ways, Hitler was the kind of forceful saviour that many of the Jews oppressed by the Romans had longed for.

Jung points to the similarities between the position of the Germans and the Jews of old. Since their humiliating defeat in World War I, the Germans awaited a saviour. "That is characteristic of people with an inferiority complex," said Jung (*C.G. Jung Speaking* 122). He sees the comparable causes of this complex in both groups as geographical and political:

> The Jews got their inferiority complex from geographical and political factors. They lived in a part of the world which was a parade ground for conquerors from both sides, and after their return from their first exile to Babylon, when they were threatened with extinction by the Romans, they invented the solacing idea of a Messiah who was going to bring all the Jews together into a nation once more and save them.

Jung continues:

> And the Germans got their inferiority complex from comparable causes. They came up out of the Danube valley too late, and founded the beginnings of their nation long after the French and the English were well on their way to nationhood. They got too late to the scramble for colonies and for the foundation of empire. Then, when they did get together and made a united nation, they looked around them and saw the British, the French, and others with rich colonies and all the equipment of grown-up nations, and they became jealous, resentful, like a younger brother whose older brothers have taken the lion's share of the inheritance. (122)

Jung explains here the *original* source of the German inferiority complex. Germany's defeat in World War I and the hard reparations required by the Treaty of Versailles did not help German egos. Humiliated and increasingly helpless as economic depression swept through the country, the German people understandably fell under the spell of Hitler, a political genius who tuned into their loss of face and their despair. Hitler offered strong leadership at a time when beggars filled the streets; he turned shame into pride, despair into hope and action. In the beginning of his career, Hitler became Germany's saviour as he mobilized the people to a sense of purpose and effected a miraculous period of prosperity.

The forceful determination and inventiveness of the masculine principle created miracles in Germany in much the same way as it has done for humanity at large. But, unbalanced by the feminine elements of empathy and compassion, the masculine ultimately led to disaster. Nowhere is this reality more evident than in Adolf Hitler's career. The way of this unbalanced charismatic dictator, unlike Christ, led to force, the heartless mass murder of innocents, and to world war. Hitler's miracle turned into an unrealistic, heartless pursuit of perfection and limitless power—compensation for an unacknowledged inferiority complex. The cost in human terms was staggering.

Hitler came along at a crucial time in history (synchronistically, perhaps, as a warning) for he was part and parcel of the dangerous degree to which the unbalanced masculine principle had advanced in our civilization. The extent of Hitler's brutality would have been impossible without the aid of modern technology. In his memoirs, Albert Speer, who fell under the satanic spell of Hitler, observes the crucial contribution of modern technology to the criminal events that took place during the Hitler era:

> The criminal events of those years were not only an outgrowth of Hitler's personality. The extent of the crimes was also due to the fact that Hitler was the first to be able to employ the implements of technology to multiply crime. (521)

Speer goes into considerable detail:

> Hitler's dictatorship was the first dictatorship of an industrial state in this age of modern technology, a dictatorship which employed to perfection the instruments of technology to dominate its own people. . . . By means of such instruments of technology as the radio and public-address systems, eighty million people could be made subject to the will of one individual. Telephone, teletype, and radio made it possible to transmit the commands of the highest levels directly to the lowest organs where because of their high authority they were executed uncritically. . . . The instruments of technology made it

> possible to maintain a close watch over all citizens and to keep criminal operations shrouded in a high degree of secrecy. To the outsider this state apparatus may look like the seemingly wild tangle of cables in a telephone exchange, but like such an exchange it could be directed by a single will. Dictatorships of the past needed assistants of high quality in the lower ranks of leadership also—men who could think and act independently. The authoritarian system in the age of technology can do without such men. The means of communication alone enable it to mechanize the work of lower leadership. Thus the type of uncritical receiver of orders is created. (520-521)

Speer footnotes the words of Harry L. Stimson (U.S. Secretary of State from 1929-33, Secretary of War from 1912-13 and 1940-45), who pointed in 1947 to the brutalization of all men under modern conditions of warfare and warned of the potential destruction of civilization:

> We must never forget that under modern conditions of life, science and technology, all war has become greatly brutalized, and that no one who joins in it, even in self-defense,

> can escape becoming also in a measure brutalized. Modern war cannot be limited in its destructive method and the inevitable debasement of all participants. . . . A fair scrutiny of the last two World Wars makes clear the steady intensification in the inhumanity of the weapons and methods employed by both the aggressors and the victors. . . . In the use of strategic air power the Allies took the lives of hundreds of thousands of civilians in Germany and in Japan. . . . We as well as our enemies have contributed to the proof that the central moral problem is war and not its methods, and that a continuance of war will in all probability end with the destruction of our civilization. (520)

We came to the edge of this destruction with Hitler. Had Germany been the first to develop the atom bomb, Hitler would certainly have used it to conquer the world. As Speer confirms, "I am sure that Hitler would not have hesitated for a moment to employ atom bombs against England" (227). It is fortunate that although Hitler had sometimes spoken to Speer about the possibility of an atom bomb, "The idea quite obviously strained his intellectual capacity," and he "was also unable to grasp the revolutionary nature of nuclear physics."

In his final speech at the Nuremberg trials, Albert Speer expressed a dire warning, similar to Stimson's, about the future:

> I thought of the consequences that unrestricted rule together with the power of technology—making use of it, but also driven by it—might have in the future. This war had ended with remote-controlled rockets, aircraft flying at the speed of sound, atom bombs, and a prospect of chemical warfare. In five to ten years it would be possible for an atomic rocket, perhaps serviced by ten men, to annihilate a million human beings in the center of New York within seconds. It would be possible to spread plagues and destroy harvests. The more technological the world becomes, the greater is the danger. . . . As the former minister in charge of a highly developed armaments economy it is my last duty to state: *A new great war will end with the destruction of human culture and civilization. There is nothing to stop unleashed technology and science from completing its work of destroying man which it has so*

terribly begun in this war. (521) (emphasis mine)

Speer was right. He notes in his memoirs, "Almost two decades later President Kennedy said at his press conference of August 20, 1963, 'What we now have . . . will kill three hundred million people in one hour'" (569). Over thirty years later, the United States, England, France, Russia, China and Israel, among others, stand in possession of enough atomic weapons to wipe out all human life on this planet.

Recently, I listened to an interview in which the great violinist and humanitarian Yehudi Menuhin expressed his grave concern about the crisis we all face. He acknowledged that we are living in a very dangerous age. As he phrased it, "The four horsemen of the apocalypse are upon us." Menuhin is one among many who is concerned about the growing universal distrust, violence and ruthlessness in our society. While he acknowledged that there is an increasing awareness of the seriousness of our situation, he confessed "I don't know what will save us."

The answer lies in the elevation of the feminine principle, that is, caring, compassionate love. We all need to be loved. While our bodies demand food for survival, our souls beg for the warmth, affirmation and connection that love provides. Without this precious element, we are out in the cold, well fed or not. Indeed, without the feeling that someone cares, we might as well be dead. As Marianne Williamson says in an audiotaped discussion, "The will of the universe is love."

The feminine nurturing principle is essentially the message of that androgynous ideal figure Jesus Christ who urged us to love our neighbors as ourselves. Christ's message went radically further to include love for one's enemies:

> You have heard that it was said, "You shall love your neighbor and hate your enemy." But I say to you, love your enemies, bless those who curse you, do good to those who hate you, and pray for those who spitefully use you and persecute you, that you may be sons of your Father in heaven; for He makes His sun rise on the evil and on the good, and sends rain on the just and on the unjust. (Matthew 5:43-45)

Few (perhaps a handful of saints) have taken Christ's message to heart and traveled this difficult path designed to eliminate violence. It takes an androgynous human being to do so. Jung pointed out that Christianity is really one man's magnificent vision for the future.

Obviously, a conscious giant leap in human evolution is urgently required as the way out of our currently diseased, unbalanced predicament. A full and honest recognition of the crucial survival value of the feminine principle is the first step toward an increase in androgynous (balanced) identities in the world. The task is difficult since we erroneously regard the feminine mode in a negative light as weak, passive and vulnerable, overlooking its yielding strength. Paradoxically, it takes great spiritual strength to accept one's fundamental weakness and vulnerability. Without this initial step, however, in our too long male-dominated society, a foundation for eventual world peace is unattainable. We must give the feminine her due place in the sun if our human species is to survive.

Bibliography

Carnes, Patrick. *Don't Call It Love: Recovery from Sexual Addiction.* New York: Bantam Books, 1991.

Deutsch, Helene. "Ein Frauenschicksal: George Sand." Almanach für das Jahr 1929. *Internat. Psychoanal.* Vienna: Verlag, 1929.

Dostoevsky, Fedor. *Crime and Punishment.* 1953. Trans. Jessie Coulson. Oxford: Oxford University Press, 1992.

Dworkin, Andrea. *Intercourse.* New York: Free Press, 1987.

Endo, Shusaku. *A Life of Jesus.* Trans. Richard A. Schuchert. New York: Paulist Press, 1973.

Freud, Sigmund. *The Future of an Illusion.* Trans. W.E. Robson-Scott. Garden City, New York: Doubleday Anchor, 1957.

García Márquez, Gabriel. *Love in the Time of Cholera.* Trans. Edith Grossman. New York: Penguin, 1989.

Gaylin, Willard, M.D. *The Male Ego.* New York: Penguin, 1992.

Gilligan, Carol. *In a Different Voice.* Cambridge, Mass.: Harvard University Press, 1982.

Greene, Graham. *Essais Catholiques.* Trans. Marcelle Sibon. Paris: Éditions du Seuil, 1953.

Holy Bible: Old and New Testaments. King James Version. Nashville: Thomas Nelson Inc., 1976.

Jung, Carl Gustav. *Memories, Dreams, Reflections.* 1961. Ed. Aniela Jaffe. Trans. Richard and Clara Winston. New York: Vintage Books/Random 1973.

Jung, Emma. *Animus and Anima.* Dallas, Texas: Spring Publications, Inc., 1957.

Kloss, Robert J. "Balancing the Hurts and Needs: Olsen' s 'I Stand Here Ironing.'" *Journal of Evolutionary Psychology. XV* (1994), 78-86.

Kohut, Heinz. *The Analysis of the Self.* New York: International Universities Press Inc., 1971.

Kramer, Jonathan, and Diane Dunaway. *Why Men Don't Get Enough Sex and Women Don't Get Enough Love.* New York, N.Y.: Pocket Books, 1990.

McGuire, William, and R.F.C. Hull, eds. *C.G. Jung Speaking: Interviews and Encounters.*

Bollingen Series XCVII. Princeton, New Jersey: Princeton University Press, 1977.

Morin, Gertrude. "Edith Stein' s Appreciation of the Feminine Function." *Journal of Evolutionary Psychology. XVII* (1996), 188-194.

Ortega y Gasset, José. "Landscape with a Deer." *On Love: Aspects of a Single Theme.* New York: Meridian, 1957.

Payne, Robert. *The Life and Death of Adolf Hitler.* New York, N.Y.: Praeger Publishers, 1973.

Phipps, William E. *Recovering Biblical Sensuousness.* Philadelphia: Westminster Press, 1975.

Potok, Chaim. *I Am the Clay.* New York: Alfred A. Knopf, 1992.

Psychiatric Dictionary. Fourth ed. Ed. Leland E. Hinsie, Robert Jean Campbell. New York: Oxford University Press, 1970.

Random House Dictionary of the English Language. Second Edition. Unabridged. New York, N.Y., 1981.

Reik, Theodor. *Of Love and Lust: On the Psychoanalysis of Romantic and Sexual Emotions.* c 1941. New York: Farrar, Strauss and Company, 1984.

Reynaud, Emmanuel. *Holy Virility: The Social Construction of Masculinity.* Trans. R. Schwartz. London: Pluto Press, 1983.

Sayers, Janet. *Mothering Psychoanalysis: Helene Deutsch, Karen Horney, Anna Freud and Melanie Klein.* London: Hamish Hamilton, 1991.

Shakespeare, William. *The Merchant of Venice. The Riverside Shakespeare.* Ed. G. Blakemore Evans. Boston: Houghton, 1974.

Shields, Carol. *The Stone Diaries.* Toronto: Random House of Canada, 1993.

Speer, Albert. *Inside the Third Reich: Memoirs.* Trans. Richard and Clara Winston. New York, N.Y.: MacMillan, 1970.

Stein, Edith. *Essays on Woman.* Vol. 2, Collected Works. Ed. Dr. L. Gelber and Romaeus Leuven OCD. Trans. Freda Mary Oben. Washington: ICS Publications, 1987.

Stern, Karl. *The Flight from Woman.* c 1965. New York: Paragon House, 1985.

Tannen, Deborah. *You Just Don't Understand: Women and Men in Conversation.* New York: Ballantine Books, 1990.

Tolstoy, Leo. *The Kreutzer Sonata.* Trans. Isai Kamen. New York: Vintage Books, 1957.

Webster's Encyclopedic Dictionary of the English Language. New York: Lexicon Publications, Inc., 1988.

Williamson, Marianne, with Anthony Robbins. *Powertalk.* Audio tape. Robbins Research International Inc. 1993, Vol. 23.

Woolf, Virginia. *To the Lighthouse.* Oxford: Oxford University Press, 1992.